D1345398

Disraeli

Disraeli

R. W. Davis

THE LIBRARY OF WORLD BIOGRAPHY
J. H. PLUMB, GENERAL EDITOR

HUTCHINSON OF LONDON

Hutchinson & Co (Publishers) Ltd
3 Fitzroy Square, London W1

London Melbourne Sydney Auckland
Wellington Johannesburg and agencies
throughout the world

First published in Great Britain 1976
© R. W. Davis 1976

Printed in Great Britain by litho by The Anchor Press Ltd
and bound by Wm Brendon & Son Ltd
both of Tiptree, Essex

ISBN 0 09 127690 X

To a perfect wife

Contents

Acknowledgments

This book has been more the product of reading and contemplation than of extensive archival research. There are still, however, several acknowledgments which must be made. One of the pleasures of writing it has been the frequent recollections of a delightful year spent in Buckinghamshire in the course of a study of its electoral politics in the eighteenth and nineteenth centuries. I remember particularly the kindness and friendship of Jack Davis and the staff at the Record Office, and the hospitality of the National Trust and its allowing me to consult the Disraeli Papers at Hughenden on this aspect of his career. On one occasion during this book I have quoted from the Tindal Papers at the Record Office. J. H. Plumb has been an inspiration, both as a great teacher and as a friend. My own students, particularly Michael Isikoff and Martin Adams, have kept my mind lively on the subject. Mr. G. Sargent has obtained for me materials it would be difficult to obtain on this side of the Atlantic. The book is dedicated to his daughter.

Introduction

WHEN WE LOOK BACK at the past nothing, perhaps, fascinates us so much as the fate of individual men and women. The greatest of these seem to give a new direction to history, to mold the social forces of their time and create a new image, or open up vistas that humbler men and women never imagined. An investigation of the interplay of human temperament with social and cultural forces is one of the most complex yet beguiling studies a historian can make; men molded by time, and time molded by men. It would seem that to achieve greatness both the temperament and the moment must fit like a key into a complex lock. Or rather a master key, for the very greatest of men and women resonate in ages distant to their own. Later generations may make new images of them — one has only to think what succeeding generations of Frenchmen have made of Napoleon, or Americans of Benjamin Franklin — but this only happens because some men change the course of history and stain it with their own ambitions, desires, creations or hopes of a magnitude that embraces future generations like a miasma. This is particularly true of the great figures of religion, of politics, of war. The great creative spirits, however, are used by subsequent generations in a reverse manner — men and women go to them to seek hope or solace, or to confirm despair, reinterpreting the works of imagination or wisdom to ease them in their own desperate necessities, to beguile them with a sense of beauty or merely to draw from them strength and understanding. So this series of biographies tries in lucid, vivid, and dramatic narratives to explain the greatness of men and women, not only how they managed to secure their niche in the great pantheon of Time, but also why they have continued to fascinate subsequent generations. It may seem, therefore, that it is paradoxical for this series to contain living men and women, as well as the dead, but it is not so. We can recognize, in our own time, particularly in those whose careers are getting close to their final hours, men and women of indisputable greatness, whose position in history is secure, and about whom the legends and myths are beginning to sprout — for all great men and women become legends, all become in history larger than their own lives.

Few careers are more remarkable than Benjamin Disraeli's. Surely Napoleon's rise to fame was more meteoric, from an obscure Corsican subaltern to Emperor of France and the arbiter of Europe. But revolutions break down social structures and create tidal waves that the gifted opportunists may ride. Benjamin Disraeli's success took place in an established, deeply status-conscious society that was by and large unthinkingly anti-Semitic. The effrontery of Disraeli, or, perhaps, more fairly, the astonishing courage of Disraeli lay in the fact that he did not join the bands of radical discontent. He never identified with the underprivileged and outsiders of nineteenth-century British society. He set about capturing the allegiance of the xenophobic country squires who were deeply suspicious of foreigners as of all innovation. The leadership of the Tory party had always been in the hands of the great landed aristocracy — dukes, earls, and gentlemen of vast acres. Benjamin Disraeli did not possess an acre at the outset of his career. His father, Isaac, was a charming, somewhat feckless literary figure, closer to Bohemia than to Belgravia. And yet Benjamin ended his life as Earl of Beaconsfield, revered by the Tory party and deeply and sincerely mourned by Queen Victoria, who regarded him not only as her best Prime Minister but as a devoted friend.

How did this obscure Jew come to dominate the richest and most hidebound political party in Great Britain: not only that but lead them to victory against the liberals, crushing the granite-willed W. E. Gladstone, the pillar of political rectitude who writhed not only under the disgrace of being beaten by Tories but the double disgrace of being crushed by Disraeli whom he regarded as a shallow and glib opportunist?

There was certainly substance in Gladstone's charge of opportunism. Disraeli never worked out a coherent political philosophy; at times he stole the programme, if not the principles, of his liberal opponents. He often improvised policy, foreign and domestic. Certainly, as in his purchase of the Suez Canal shares, through the good offices of his friends the Rothschilds, he was an opportunist — but a brilliant one. No one could call him a hard-working, dedicated politician even when Prime Minister. He took long weekends, left a great deal of legislative effort to the members of his cabinet, and initiated very little policy himself. No one could say that Disraeli succeeded by dominating intellectually the political issues of the day by the thoroughness of his understanding of them. His knowledge was frequently as shallow as his views were changeable. Gladstone was right; that made Disraeli's success all the more galling.

What then were Disraeli's gifts? They were these — immense charm, great rhetoric, and an unerring political instinct for the feasible. Charm dies with the charmer. The set lines of his face do not reveal it. We know that his personal style in clothes, in the dressing of his hair, in perfume and in jewelry bordered on the vulgar. Certainly he charmed women more easily than men: Queen Victoria adored him; nonetheless, men were not immune to his charm. His conversation was brilliant and although his manners were ornate, they were also flattering. He enhanced life wherever he might be — in the boudoir or the cabinet. Gladstone by the very weight of his innate moral gravity combined with the power of his intellect could be socially depressing and stop the easy flow of dinner table gossip whereas Disraeli could set it alight. Yet there was more to Disraeli's social triumph than charm. The fact that he was a Jew and despised helped. The surprise of his charm, the amazement at being captivated often led to overcompensation. Disraeli was subtle enough to be aware of this and helped his listeners on the way to total acceptance not only by making a claim that he was an active practising Christian but also by hints of his Venetian aristocratic origins. (They did not exist.) Instead of being an outsider they discovered that he was, albeit foreign, one of them.

Disraeli possessed also an unmatchable capacity for political rhetoric. Gladstone could sway audiences through his moral fervour. But Disraeli was a great phrase maker. He knew how to touch the nerve of the nation. Again he knew how to harness jingoistic imperial aspirations in a way that Gladstone was powerless to do because he despised the emotion. Disraeli despised nothing except, perhaps, moral fervour! In his speeches in Parliament and on the hustings Disraeli knew how to play on the political hopes of the country that he had come to rule; the hopes of both the ruling elite and the voting poor.

And he had a matchless sense of timing — the right political moment for successful action. He could never have blundered as Gladstone did over Home Rule for Ireland, raising the issue long before it was feasible and in consequence courting disaster. Whereas Disraeli, indifferent to Parliamentary Reform, sensed that Reform must come in 1867 and seized his chance. The infuriated Gladstone called this opportunism, perhaps it would be better and more Disraelian to call it the exploitation of the art of the possible.

And then we must add one other dimension to Disraeli which also makes him one of the great men of nineteenth-century Europe. He was the only man to combine the office of Prime Minister with that of a distinguished professional novelist. *Coningsby, Sybil* and his other novels are books that are still read not only for the insight they give into their time but also for pleasure. His life in its daring, in its achievement and indeed in the contribution that he made to the political life of England and its Empire makes fascinating reading. And Richard Davis has written a biography of great insight. He does not spare Disraeli — the financial chicanery, the subterfuges, or the opportunism. Survival was all to Disraeli. He survived and triumphed and the story of how he did it is fascinating reading.

— J. H. PLUMB

Disraeli

ONE

The Making of the Man

As ANYONE who has ever made a leisurely way on foot from the Public Record Office to the British Museum knows, that part of London is one of those most richly endowed with green enclaves. And though, today, Holborn makes a harsh modern intrusion through the center, the gardens of the Inns of Court and the squares of the Bedfords's Bloomsbury estate continue to give it a distinct flavor. It was here that Disraeli grew to manhood.

He was born on 21 December 1804 in a house in King's Road (now 22 Theobald's Road, W.C.1) overlooking the gardens of Gray's Inn. It was not a long walk to the British Museum, where his father Isaac D'Israeli, the scion of a more than comfortably wealthy Jewish family, spent his days searching out literary and historical material for the books that made him in his own time a well-known and respected critic, essayist, and historian.

Isaac fitted the popular conception of the scholar, mild, absent-minded, and distracted from what the uninitiated call real life, completely absorbed in his masses of notes. To a little boy he doubtless seemed distant and aloof. But, though Disraeli was never to feel that his father completely understood him, he always adored him; and his letters to and about his father always breathe an unmistakable affection.

His mother was a different matter. The mention of her is rare, almost always forced, and often prompted by his tactful sister Sarah. Maria (or Miriam) Basevi also came from a wealthy and talented Jewish family. The clearest impression one gets of her, however, is of a down-to-earth, nononsense kind of person who did not hesitate to deliver good home truths when she felt it necessary. Her most significant recorded essay into Disraeli's life was in his youthful scrape with the publisher John Murray, when she was in effect to rebuke an old fool for being taken in by a young one. It was loyal, but perhaps not very lovable. Given her husband's absorption in his scholarship, her common sense was doubtless a useful commodity; but it did not endear her to her eldest son. And with a family of other young children — Sarah born in 1802, Napthali born and died in 1807, Ralph born in 1809, and James in 1813 — very probably she had less time than she might otherwise have had to devote to him. At any rate, it is clear that he never liked her; and it is perhaps not too much to speculate that the only mother in his novels who has much breath of reality, the quarrelsome and carping Mrs. Cardurcis in *Venetia,* was modeled on his own.

Lively and intelligent children who feel ignored by their parents are likely to strive all the harder to achieve recognition, and an aggressiveness is often the result. In Disraeli's case, a pugnacious nature was almost certainly strengthened by the circumstance of his being born a Jew. Lord Blake (though he shows elsewhere that he is well aware of the importance of this factor) in one instance quotes approvingly a remark by the Duke of Argyll to demonstrate that the disadvantages imposed by Disraeli's origins should not be overemphasized. It was ridiculous, the Duke contended, to talk of him "as a mere 'Jew Boy' who by the force of nothing but extraordinary genius attained to the leadership of a great party." It was not the want of external advantages, he argued, that stood in Disraeli's way, but his own fantastic opinions. Admittedly Disraeli's family had the advantages of comfortable wealth and a certain distinction, but the remark heightens rather than otherwise the disadvantages imposed by his Jewishness. Perhaps his contemporaries did not think of him as a *"mere* 'Jew Boy,' "but that hardly very affectionate term was probably never very far from the minds of most. And, while rich or otherwise powerful Jews could undoubtedly achieve a grudging acceptance in nineteenth-century English society, little Benjamin was clearly neither.

Disraeli himself later said that he had been raised in ignorance of, and even hostility toward, the traditions of the Jewish people. Certainly, as Philip Guedalla has remarked, there is nothing in his written work that would indicate any greater knowledge about the history of his people than a reasonable familiarity with the Old Testament would provide. There is evidence, however, that at the Reverend Mr. Potticany's in Blackheath, which would have been roughly the equivalent of the modern English prep school in his education, he and another Jewish boy stood at the back of the room during prayers, and that they both received instruction from a rabbi who visited on Saturdays. Even had there not been these formal evidences of his differentness, Disraeli's appearance, his dark and aquiline features, would have set him apart. As other biographers have remarked, Contarini Fleming's experiences in Disraeli's early novel of the same name, Contarini's sense of looking and being different, and his descriptions of the schoolboy fights that grew out of his differentness are pretty clearly autobiographical.

Isaac would not have encouraged any Jewish proclivities in his son. Isaac's own opinions were of the kind of Voltairian skepticism which had been fashionable on the continent before the French Revolution, when he had rounded off his education there. But probably out of deference to the opinions of his father, Benjamin I, an amiable stock-broker, Isaac maintained a formal connection with the Sephardic (the family was predominantly Italian in origin) congregation of Bevis Marks. In 1813, however, he was elected parnass, or warden, of the congregation. Isaac considered this too much of a travesty, and refused. Whereupon, as was also common practice with onerous parish offices in the civil sphere, he was fined. He refused to pay the fine. The quarrel simmered on until 1817, when Benjamin I died, and Isaac put an end to the matter by insisting that his name be erased from the list of members. Thus ended the family's formal connection with the Jewish religion.

Isaac never bothered to establish a connection with any other, but his friend Sharon Turner, well known by his contemporaries as an historian of Anglo-Saxon England, persuaded him to go further in the case of his children. The reason was a worldly one, and of immense significance for young Benjamin's future career. Since the reign of Charles II the Test and Corporation Acts, though passed primarily to exclude Protestant Dissenters* and Catholics, had excluded all who did not conform to the Church of England from civil and military offices, from the universities, and from some professions. The legal theory was not always reflected in actual practice, but it was more often than historians generally have believed. In any event, there can be little doubt that by creating a second-class citizenry, even if it were sometimes in theory only, the law perpetuated prejudice and in this way posed a barrier to social and civic equality. In 1828 and 1829 the law was to be abrogated for the most part for Dissenters and Catholics respectively. But a declaration which was then required of all officeholders and members of Parliament, "on the true faith of a Christian," perpetuated the bar for Jews. Had Disraeli

---

* That is, Presbyterians, Congregationalists, Baptists, Unitarians, and later Methodists. Quakers tended to be in a separate category, though the term applies broadly to all non-Anglican Protestants.

remained one he would never have attained the heights of political power.

But he did not. On 31 July 1817, shortly after his brothers and before his sister, he was received into the Anglican faith. Some have seen significance in the month that elapsed between Benjamin and his brothers, suggesting reluctance on his part; but there is no evidence to support such a theory, or to suggest that he did not settle comfortably into a faith that has never been overly demanding or searching into the individual conscience.

In the same year the family moved to 6 Bloomsbury Square, nearer the British Museum, and the thirteen-year-old Benjamin changed his school. Like his former school, this one was run by a Dissenting minister. It was at the end of the great days of the Dissenting academies, which for most of the eighteenth century had provided the highest quality education to young men of every creed. The Reverend Eli Cogan of Higham Hall, near Walthamstow in Epping Forest, was, like many of his predecessors, of the intellectual Unitarian persuasion, and his school was highly thought of. In his two years or so there, the young Disraeli acquired a fairly good grasp of Latin and a much more shaky one of Greek. More important in his own memory of his school days, he believed that he had been exposed to English public school life in the small. Since boys left to themselves — though mercifully they were left less to themselves at the Reverend Mr. Cogan's than at one of the great public schools — tend to perpetrate much the same kind of barbarities on one another, he was probably right. The school did him no obvious harm, and by endowing him with a smattering of classical education, a social and political necessity at the time, it did him a positive good.

His real education, however, he attained in his father's library. There he pursued his reading of the classics, and broadened his interests to more modern works of philosophy and history. He never had much taste for the belles lettres — save insofar as what he himself wrote could be so described. As he later said, when he wanted to read a novel he wrote one! But he undoubtedly put his time to good use, particularly in acquiring an unusual grasp of modern history.

In November 1821 this leisurely mode of education was ended by his being articled to a firm of solicitors in the City, Messrs. Swain, Stevens, Maples, Pearse, and Hunt, of Frederick's Place, Old Jewry. They had a large and lucrative business, and it was the kind of secure, respectable position that many fathers dream of for their children. It was perhaps a rather peculiar choice for Isaac, who had himself successfully rebelled against similar ambitions on the part of his own parents. But Disraeli tells us that his father "was very warm about this business: the only time in his life in which he exerted authority, always, however, exerted with affection." Fathers, however, very often eschew for their children risks that they themselves have taken; and, unlike Isaac himself, Benjamin was not an only child and would have to divide his patrimony. Disraeli goes on to say, "I had some scruples, for even then I dreamed of Parliament." "Scruples" was probably putting it mildly; but he may well have been accurate about his dreams of Parliament, for what is evident about him from the earliest period of his life is his soaring ambition.

In *Vivian Grey,* his first novel, published a few years later, Disraeli says that "in England, personal distinction is the only passport to the society of the great. Whether this distinction arise from fortune, family or talent is immaterial; but certain it is, to enter into high society, a man must either have blood, a million, or a genius." "Blood" he did not have, but he was not long in beginning to experiment with the other two ingredients in the formula. For he was determined to enter into the society of the great; and for the next decade or so, until he had achieved his goal, he was to pursue entrance with singleminded determination.

One element, generally underestimated, in his final success soon became apparent, his dandyism. The wife of one

of the partners of Frederick's Place was somewhat taken
aback that he came to her house in "a black velvet suit
with ruffles, and black stockings with red clocks — which in
those days was rather conspicuous attire." Doubtless it was
not the way for a young lawyer to get ahead, but elsewhere
it would have done no harm at all. Quite the contrary. Extravagant attire by itself would never have gained social
success. But in the easy society of late Georgian and early
Victorian England, when the raffish were still powerful, it
was not a bad form of self-advertisement for someone with
other talents. Disraeli himself certainly thought it useful.
Vivian Grey, he tells us, was "an elegant lively lad with
just enough of dandyism to preserve him from committing
gaucheries and with the devil of a tongue." It was a model
he was to follow with some success.

Disraeli's pursuit of a million was not only not successful,
but a complete disaster, setting in train a series of financial
scrapes that were to plague the greater part of his life. He
later claimed that, as private secretary to one of the partners, and hence the witness to the business coups and high
finance that took place within that important man's cham-
bers, he had gained "no inconsiderable knowledge of human nature." However that may be, he seems to have
gained little knowledge of business or finance. Or perhaps
he was a living example of a little knowledge being a dangerous thing. At any rate, like many others, he suffered
grievously in the speculative boom that followed the liberal
foreign secretary's, George Canning's, recognition of the
South American republics. Starting with very little in November 1824, by June 1825, at the ripe old age of twenty,
he was several thousand pounds in debt.

To his service as a private secretary Disraeli also attributed the acquiring of "great facility with my pen." This
talent was now put to public use, if not benefit, in the cause
of some of the stocks in which he was speculating. John
Powles, the head of a financial house that had been profiting from the boom, and a client of Messrs. Swain, required

a puff of one of the South American mining companies he was promoting. Disraeli produced a shameless one, under the guise of a disinterested "Enquiry into the Plans, Progress, and Policy of the American Mining Companies." It emerged in March 1825 as a pamphlet of almost a hundred pages, brought out on commission by Isaac's close friend John Murray. This, Disraeli's first published work, hardly reflected well on him, or on anyone else involved in the venture. Two others of a similar nature followed in quick succession.

Needless to say, he had been almost entirely ignorant of the facts of the situation, as his own disastrous losses proved. But ignorance did not deter him either from an even more bizarre venture, which is not less mystifying in that men of considerable sophistication and experience appear to have been completely taken in by him. Firmly mired in debt by his speculations, in July of 1825 he decided to recoup his losses, and soar to power and influence, as the publisher of a new morning paper to be devoted to the political cause of George Canning. In this venture he was once again joined by Powles and John Murray.

The partners had grandiose plans. Sir Walter Scott was kindly disposed to Canning, and had been associated with Murray in the influential Tory organ the *Quarterly Review*. Even Disraeli and his new associates did not believe that they could secure the great Sir Walter as their editor, but they set their sights on his son-in-law, J. G. Lockhart. Disraeli was sent up to Scotland to conduct the negotiations, and found Lockhart at his cottage near his father-in-law's famous seat at Abbotsford. The young emissary's reports make it evident that there were few limits to his imagined success. As befitted the importance of his mission, he wrote with code names. He reported that "M.," as Lockhart was called, was "fully aware that he may end by making his situation as important as any in the empire." He was confident that "The Chevalier [Sir Walter] entered into it excellently." He went on to make suggestions for the handling of the final negotiations:

> When M. comes to town, it will be most important that it should be distinctly proved to him that he *will* be supported by the great interests I have mentioned to him. He must see that, through Powles, all America and the Commercial Interest is at our beck . . . ; that the West India Interest will pledge themselves; that such men and in such situations as Barrow [Secretary of the Admiralty], &c., &c., are *distinctly in our power;* and, finally, that he is coming to London, not to be an Editor of a Newspaper, but the Director-General of an immense organ, and at the head of a band of high-bred gentlemen and important interests.

He asked his friends in London to arrange for a parliamentary seat for Lockhart, through one of their alleged confidants in the government. "If this point could be arranged, I have no doubt that I shall be able to organise, in the interest with which I am now engaged, a most *immense party,* and a *most serviceable one.*"

It was, of course, arrant nonsense. But the scheme got a surprisingly long way. Lockhart, though neither he nor Sir Walter felt that he could agree to become editor of a mere newspaper, agreed in effect to do the job for the editorship of the *Quarterly Review* and a handsome salary; and magnificent plans went on apace. But here powerful former contributors to the *Quarterly,* including the influential Tory politician John Wilson Croker (whom Disraeli was later to pillory in *Coningsby*), entered the scene with a strong protest against Lockhart's appointment as editor. Murray weakened under the pressure, and in the resulting bickering with Lockhart and Scott tried to put all the blame on Disraeli, which was certainly unfair. Matters were finally patched up. Lockhart came to London in December, and the *Representative,* as the paper was called at Disraeli's suggestion, ultimately came out. It had a life of half a year and cost Murray £26,000. But Disraeli's connection with the paper had ceased before it ever appeared. The December crash of the market ended even his hopes, as well as any possibility that might have existed that he could produce his part of the capital.

This incident provided the occasion for Maria D'Israeli's delivery of some of her home truths. She told an angry Murray that "the failure of *The Representative* lay much more with the proprietor and his editor than it ever did with my son." She reminded him that he had known Benjamin from his earliest childhood, and must have been aware of his lack of resources. She went on to say that her son, though "a clever boy," was "no prodigy." Yet Murray "had formed in his versatile imagination a perfect being and expected impossibilities, and found him on trial a mere mortal and a very very young man." About Murray's gullibility, and he was not alone, she was certainly right. She may also have been right about her son. But particularly given his personality it is not hard to see how he might have found her judgments on him wounding.

It will probably come as no surprise that by this time Disraeli had long since ended any serious connection with the solicitor's profession. In the summer of 1824 both the D'Israelis, father and son (though, in fact, the latter had been spelling his name in the new way for about a year), were ill; and Isaac took his son and a young friend, William Meredith, recently down from Oxford, on a six weeks' tour of what is now Belgium, the Rhine Valley, and Luxemburg. It was on this trip that the younger Disraeli decided to abandon his late career and Isaac finally acquiesced, though the formal connection lingered on for a while. The trip also provided Disraeli with the beginning of a stock of material on foreign travel which he was to incorporate, mostly with rather unfortunate effect, in the productions of his new profession of novelist.

And his travels were not all that he was to incorporate. During the autumn of 1825, when the negotiations over the

Representative were in full swing, Isaac rented Hyde House, near Amersham. Its owner, Robert Plumer Ward, who was a minor politician and a friend of Canning, had in the previous year published the first important "novel of fashionable life," as they were then called, or "silver fork novels," as they have since been called, and had succeeded in giving the genre some popularity. Disraeli decided to emulate his father's landlord, and it was at Hyde House that he at least began (though he probably did not finish before his twenty-first birthday, as he later boasted) his novel *Vivian Grey*, modeled on Plumer Ward's *Tremaine*. The great difference between the two was that, while the author of the latter knew something of the life of the great and powerful, the author of the former knew very little. Disraeli's knowledge was pretty much limited to the kind of people who would have frequented the dinner tables of his father and John Murray; and the latter personage, transformed into a tipsy nobleman, figured all too prominently in the novel. Murray was furious, and had good reason to be.

Save in the famous trilogy,* a common characteristic of all Disraeli's novels is their cynical and opportunistic view of life in general, and politics in particular. The pained conclusion of Archbishop Tait of the last novel, *Endymion,* that the "writer considers all political life as mere play and gambling," applies as well to the first. *Vivian Grey* does not, it is true, have the carefully developed setting, closely related to actual political men and events, of the later "political" novels. But it is nonetheless mainly about politics. The story is basically a simple one. Vivian is a young man of genius, but of a family that, though respectable, is neither wealthy nor distinguished, save by his father's literary achievements. How was genius to triumph? The author answered the question by posing another: "At this

---

* *Coningsby, Sybil,* and *Tancred,* the ostensible message of which, as will be seen, the author himself was far from taking entirely seriously.

moment how many a powerful noble wants only wit to be a Minister, and what wants Vivian Grey to attain the same end? That noble's influence." The peer who was to play this honorable role was the vain, stupid, guzzling Marquis of Carabas, modeled on the unfortunate Murray. For most of the book, Vivian carries all before him, to be foiled in the end only by what in more edifying circumstances might be called cruel and capricious fate. In disgrace, he then retires to Germany, where, in a portion of the book written and published as another installment, the reader is treated to what is little more than a travelogue. Publishing in installments was then the custom, but the latter parts usually bore some relation to those that preceded.

The interest, however, is in the main body of the work. It certainly does not lie in its literary appeal, for of that there is very little. For the general modern audience, Disraeli's novels would make very heavy going indeed. And, though some students of literature have tried to ascribe to them an importance in the history of ideas they probably do not possess, literary scholars generally avoid them. In any case, *Vivian Grey* is short, to say the least, on ideas. Nor, as has been suggested, does the novel have much of the minutiae of politics, or of political polemic as opposed to ideas, which some of the later novels have and which must be interesting to historians. But to the biographer it is full of portent. That the novel is autobiographical at the most superficial level is too obvious a point to need belaboring. It also has a much deeper significance. Disraeli himself later confided to his diary that "my works are the embodification of my feelings. In *Vivian Grey* I have portrayed my active and real ambition." His apologists have argued that this should not be taken very seriously, since the "moral" — or perhaps one should say the "immoral" — of most of the tale is simply too outrageous to be taken at face value. One could argue, to the contrary, that it is precisely when Disraeli is at his most outrageous that one is likely to get nearest to his

real beliefs. And no one who follows closely his next few
years, and indeed his whole life, can seriously doubt the
genuineness of sentiment in the words he puts into Vivian's
mouth:

> I am no cold-blooded philosopher that would despise that for
> which, in my opinion, men, real men, should alone exist.
> Power! Oh! what sleepless nights, what days of hot anxiety!
> what exertions of mind and body! what travel! what hatred!
> what fierce encounters! what dangers of all possible kinds,
> would I not endure with a joyous spirit to gain it!

It was to be the story of his life.

Ostensibly a novel about high life published anony-
mously by an insider, the book was at first a great success.
The success was undoubtedly assisted by the wife of Plumer
Ward's solicitor, Sarah Austen, herself something of a blue-
stocking and minor patroness of literary talent, who served
as Disraeli's confidante and adviser and probably helped to
give the book some of the style of *Tremaine*. She also secured Plumer Ward's publisher, Colburn, who in his turn
helped with some superb puffing. But most of all the book
owed its success to the vanity and obsession with self of
most of mankind. High society needed only to be told that
the book was about themselves, and they believed it. And,
as has happened with later books about Cambridge colleges
and other places, men imagined they saw themselves where
they were not. It was inevitable that, as Disraeli knew nothing of high society, most who recognized themselves would
be wrong. Indeed, save for his father, who was flatteringly
portrayed, probably only Murray, who was certainly not
high society, would have been right.

Finally a critic pointed out the obvious. All the other
critics leapt on the bandwagon and said things in the un-
kind way that critics have. High society was naturally
furious at having been fooled. Murray was furious because
he had not been. And the world in general heaped obloquy

on Disraeli. Coming on top of his other disasters, it was a doubly shattering experience. Disraeli turned for solace, as he almost always would, to an older woman.

As Professor Jerman was the first to make clear, in his work on those aspects of the young Disraeli's career which the respectable and discreet Mr. Monypenny thought best to let alone, Disraeli always craved, and received, mothering, even from his one young mistress, Henrietta Sykes. And it is evident that maternal care was much more important to him than any sexual relationship. It will be remembered, after all, that the famous compliment to Mrs. Disraeli — "Why, my dear, you are more like a mistress than a wife" — was occasioned by no more than a bottle of champagne and a pie from Fortnum and Mason's. Most men would expect more from their mistresses, and even their wives. This is not to say that Disraeli disliked sex, or was in any way incapable of it, and indeed later evidence shows that he was quite capable of entering into all the dissipations with which young rakes diverted themselves; but his appetites were moderate. There is no evidence that Sarah Austen was ever his mistress in any sexual sense. But she did exercise what Disraeli was later to celebrate as the feminine inspiration (he meant love, devotion, and encouragement) that stood behind every great man.

In June 1826 the Austens took the depressed and ailing young author off to the continent for a holiday. They went to Paris and then to Geneva. There Disraeli was able to indulge in worship of the memory of a man who was a hero to many of his young contemporaries, Byron. His admiration was probably greater in that Byron, for reasons not entirely evident to a modern reader, had professed himself an admirer of the gentle Isaac's literary compilations. Byron himself, of course, was gentle in neither word nor deed; and, to Disraeli's great joy, he was able to emulate one of the poet's feats celebrated in *Childe Harold,* being taken out by Byron's own boatman during a violent thunderstorm on the lake. The travelers then proceeded to northern Italy, taking in Milan, Verona, Vicenza, and then Venice. There, oddly enough, though he admired the city, we find no allusion to the fantastic aristocratic Venetian ancestry he was later to claim for himself. Bologna and Florence followed, and then home by way of Turin and the Rhone Valley. Once again, his experiences and impressions would be recorded, not entirely to the benefit of his later novels.

They arrived home late in October. The trip had given Disraeli a respite, but it had not cured his deep depression; and for the next two years he sank into what would today be described as a nervous breakdown. These years are largely blank. There is the occasional word of Disraeli's doings. In November 1824, probably to satisfy Isaac's lingering desire for a legal career for his son, he had entered his name at Lincoln's Inn, which ought to have led in the ordinary course of events to his ultimately being called to the Bar. It was certainly not Disraeli's own preference. His opinion of the legal profession had been succinctly stated in *Vivian Grey:* "THE BAR — pooh! law and bad jokes till we are forty; and then with the most brilliant success the prospect of gout and a coronet." And, though he paid his dues and ate his dinners (he always liked his food) through these years, there is no sign that he did anything else toward furthering his supposed career. He was probably incapable of doing much. In the summer of 1827 there is a report that he is seriously ill at Fyfield, in Oxfordshire, where his family were spending their holidays in the company of the Austens. In the summer of 1828 he was ill again, this time at Lyme Regis.

The source of his difficulty was not far to seek. In March he had written to Sharon Turner:

I am at present quite idle, being at this moment slowly recovering from one of those tremendous disorganizations which happen to all men at some period of their lives, and which are perhaps equally necessary for the formation of both body and constitution. Whether I shall ever do anything which may mark me out from the crowd, I know not. I am one of those

to whom moderate reputation can give no pleasure, and who
in all probability am incapable of achieving a great one.

Whether all men suffer such tortures is perhaps doubtful,
but those who have never forget them. The demon ambition, from which even modern youth seems not wholly immune, is often a cruel companion.

Disraeli was not entirely incapable of activity during this
period. *The Voyage of Captain Popanilla,* which he had
probably begun several years before, came out in the spring
of 1828. It was a satire reminiscent of writings of Swift and
Voltaire, taking off Jeremy Bentham and his Utilitarian
disciples as a starter, and then going on to pay the same
compliment to English social and political institutions generally. The future leader of the Protectionist party heaped
scorn upon the Corn Laws, the founder of Imperialism
roasted the Colonial system (which, as it happened, were
also bugbears of the Utilitarians). He attacked Utilitarian-
ism for being ahistorical, but it was by no means evident
what the rest of society had gained from the lessons of history.

But bursts of activity were followed by recurring bouts of
depression. His son's low state appears to have been one of
the considerations that determined Isaac to move his family
once for all into quiet rural Buckinghamshire. "The precarious health of several members of my family," he wrote
to Robert Southey, the poet, "has decided me on this
movement, and I quit London with all its hourly seduc-
tions. My house is described by the 'Nourrise of Antiqui-
ties,' venerable Camden, as built by the Lord Windsor in
the reign of Henry VIII — for the salubrity of soil and air."
In fact, the style of the ample red-brick mansion that stood
there then, and now, was of the reign of Queen Anne. The
little village of Bradenham sat as it does still, tucked in the
Chiltern hillside overlooking the road toward Princes Ris-
borough and Aylesbury, not far from where it branches off
the A.40 between Wycombe and West Wycombe. It is re-

markably little changed. The manor house, with its neighboring church, still dominates the village. The modern
sprawl of High Wycombe is hidden by an arm of the hills,
and the house still looks over a green and pleasant valley.
The hillside behind remains covered with beeches and firs,
with Naphill Common and its stretches of turf and heather
beyond. It is a beautiful spot, and Disraeli loved it and the
surrounding Chiltern countryside from the beginning. For
Isaac it must have been an awful wrench to leave the British Museum; but he was comforted by his own splendid
library, which was ultimately to follow his son in the short
move across the hills to Hughenden.

For nearly twelve months the young Disraeli rarely left
Bradenham, and during this period his spirits began to revive. His mind turned to a new project for a book, the life
of David Alroy, a Jewish hero of the twelfth century, an
idea which was in due course to come to fruition as a novel.
He began as well to yearn to see some of the lands where
Alroy had triumphed, and others made popular by the ad-
ventures of Byron and the foreign policy of Canning. He
began to hanker, in short, for a Near Eastern tour. The
difficulty was that travel cost money. Not only did he have
none, but, as more and more was borrowed at exorbitant
rates to fend off his creditors, his burden of debt grew. Yet,
though his debts annoyed him, Disraeli's was not the kind
of temperament to sink under their weight. It was during
this very period that he first began to talk cheerfully about
buying himself a country estate; and, when his mind became set on travel, he set about with a will the process of
scraping together the money. Isaac would not pay. And so,
as "go I must," he gaily told Austen, "I fear I must hack for
it." He had, according to him, never before been a "literary
prostitute." His mining pamphlets might throw doubt on
that assertion, but there can be no doubt that a literary
prostitute is what he now became.

The Young Duke, published in 1831, was written for
money. It was about a young nobleman who, partly through

vast expenditures, became the lion of society. The other part of the explanation of his success was that he played to the hilt the role of the dandy. Impudence, the author tells us, gets one far in society. There are no weapons like the "spear of sarcasm" and the "shield of nonchalance." The dandy is the most important of individuals, and so on. Disraeli believed this, or much of it, and put his belief into practice. Henry Bulwer, later ambassador to Washington and Constantinople, remembered attending a dinner party at his brother's house in the spring of 1830, where Disraeli appeared in "green velvet trousers, a canary coloured waistcoat, low shoes, silver buckles, lace at his wrists, and his hair in ringlets. . . . If on leaving the table we had been severally asked which was the cleverest of the party we should have been obliged to say 'the man in the green velvet trousers.' " Henry's brother was Edward Lytton Bulwer, like Disraeli a novelist; and it was Lytton Bulwer, who had the advantage of also being the scion of an old and distinguished Hertfordshire family, who was to be mainly responsible for Disraeli's successful launching into society.

Like his creator, the young duke was to get far by such means. Also reminiscent of his creator, he came close to being ruined by a burden of debt. He was rescued and rehabilitated by a virtuous Catholic gentleman and his daughter. And the young duke's redemption was marked by his attending the House of Lords and delivering an impassioned plea for the removal of Catholic disabilities, the arguments on both sides of which burning question Disraeli made it quite evident elsewhere in the book he considered ridiculous. For good measure, he also reiterated his contempt for the Utilitarians and their "Screw and Lever Review," as he unkindly dubbed the *Westminster Review*. Disraeli later claimed that it was a moral tale, but once again it is the amorality that is a good deal more evident.

At any rate, it did the trick so far as Disraeli was concerned. Colburn paid him £500 for the book. This was a good start toward the cost of his projected trip. The rest he did not hesitate to borrow from Austen, whose money Disraeli still considered good, though the charms of his wife had begun to pale. He was thus saved from the fate he had earlier decried of being "pointed out as the young gentleman who *was* going to Constantinople." And Austen himself turned out to be the "friendly breeze" that he hoped would blow him to Syria.

It is impossible in a short space to do justice to the tour which lasted from the end of May 1830 to October 1831. Disraeli's traveling companion was the same William Meredith who had accompanied him on his first tour of the continent in 1824, and the bond between them had since been made closer by Meredith's engagement to Sarah Disraeli. Together they dodged bandits in Spain, and Disraeli shocked and fascinated the garrisons of Gibraltar and Malta by his extravagant dress and behavior. In Malta they fell in with James Clay, who had been at Winchester with Ralph Disraeli and at Oxford with Meredith. Disraeli at any rate entered with zest into the dissipations of this fraternal acquaintance, drinking and whoring with the best. From the latter activity he acquired the not uncommon complaint which in those days was treated only with doses of mercury, successfully in his case.

Toward the end of September they sailed as guests on Clay's yacht to Corfu, and thence to Yanina, the capital of Turkish Albania. The Turks had been engaged in one of their periodic massacres of subject peoples, and Disraeli was bent on joining the conquering army as a volunteer. But they had done their job too well, and the rebellion had been crushed by the time he arrived. So he had had to content himself with merely paying a visit to the Grand Vizier, and experiencing "the delight of being made much of by a man who was daily decapitating half the Province."

Such cynicism is evidently too outrageous to be taken seriously. Disraeli, however, was always inclined to be skeptical of what other people saw as atrocities. And his pro-Turkish prejudices, contrasting sharply with the pro-Greek sentiments of Byron and what passed for British public opinion generally, were only confirmed by his travels. "I am quite a Turk," he wrote to Austen, "wear a turban, smoke a pipe six feet long, and squat on a divan."

Still, he was dazzled by Athens and thoroughly enjoyed the Greek tour which followed the Albanian sojourn. They then sailed on to Constantinople, which needless to say he adored. Meredith did not stay so long as his companions, going overland to Smyrna at the beginning of the year. Clay and Disraeli followed on the yacht a couple of weeks later, but finding their friend bent on an expedition inland to "the unseen relics of some unheard-of cock-and-a-bull city," they continued to sail southward toward their next objective, the Holy Land.

Jerusalem did not belie Disraeli's high expectations, and he placed it on a par with Athens. The week he spent there was, he said, "the most delightful of all our travels." But his tastes seem to have been catholic, and what apparently struck him most was the Mosque of Omar, not because it stood on the supposed site of the temple of his forefathers, but because of its own Saracenic splendor. Indeed, so struck was he that he tried to steal in in disguise, which was not successful and could have been fatal. He managed to escape from the guardians of the mosque, however, and at least "caught a glorious glimpse of splendid courts, and light airy gates. . . ."

From Jerusalem the two companions returned to the yacht which was anchored at Jaffa, and continued their journey to Egypt. In "the ancient land of Priestcraft and of Pyramids," which was another great object of fascination to Disraeli, he spent more than four months. He took in the main attractions, visiting the pyramids and sailing up the Nile. Cairo he found a "luxurious and pleasant place." In those days of restricted foreign travel, tourists were given more select treatment than they are nowadays, and Disraeli had several audiences of the pasha, with whom he discussed the mysteries of parliamentary government. But there were annoyances and worse as well. Clay, who had looked after the practical details of the trip, and told Meredith that Disraeli was one of those people who "ought never to travel without a nurse," was ill and getting ready to leave him. Meredith joined him at the end of June, but not for long. Just as they were about to start their homeward journey, his brother-in-law-to-be was stricken with smallpox, and died on 19 July.

No one can doubt Disraeli's genuine affection for his sister, but even his sympathy was of the strangely self-centered sort which was typical of him:

> Oh! my sister, in this hour of overwhelming affliction my thoughts are only for you. Alas! my beloved, if you are lost to me where, where am I to fly for refuge? I have no wife, I have no betrothed. . . . Live then, my heart's treasure for one who has ever loved you with a surpassing love, and who would cheerfully have yielded his own existence to have saved you the bitterness of this letter. Yes, my beloved, be my genius, my solace, my companion, my joy.

To a large extent, Sarah was to be what he desired, providing the female love and encouragement he always craved and required, and by her practical sense and great tact seeing him over many difficult periods thereafter. That "the perfect love of a sister and a brother" proved not to be enough for him was at least in part because she also shouldered the burden of her aging parents, and could not devote all her time to him. But she nonetheless remained until her death in 1859 a great bulwark and support. Again, the brother's fond memory was typical. His solicitor and close friend, Philip Rose, remembered remarking to him on the occasion of his first becoming Prime Minister that it was a pity his sister had not lived to see his triumph; "and he replied, 'Ah, poor Sa, poor Sa! we've lost our audience, we've lost our audience.'"

Disraeli had intended to return home by way of Naples and Rome; but he abandoned these plans, and at once set sail for England by the same route he had come. He arrived late in October 1831, at the height of agitation after the Lords' rejection of the Great Reform Bill. But politics were not to be his main concern for a while. After comforting the grieving household at Bradenham, he concentrated on his literary pursuits and on not altogether unconnected social climbing.

He had not been entirely idle during the last months of his Eastern tour and on the voyage home, and by the time of his return he had two books well under way, *Contarini Fleming,* published in 1832, and *The Wondrous Tale of Alroy,* published in 1833. In the same diary entry in which he recorded his interpretation of *Vivian Grey,* Disraeli went on to say that in *Alroy* he had portrayed his "ideal ambition," and in *Contarini Fleming* his "poetic character." What he meant by his "ideal ambition" has, not surprisingly, puzzled critics and biographers. Alroy was a twelfth-century prince of the Jews of Asia Minor, which by then had come under the rule of the Turks. He set out to reestablish the greatness of Solomon and of Jerusalem, and so long as he remained true to his goal of a revived Jewish state he prospered and conquered. But he became seduced by the fleshpots of Baghdad, modern-day Babylon, into grand schemes of conquest, and of establishing an eclectic and tolerant empire over the whole Middle East. The result was failure and disgrace. The difficulty is that, as so often with Disraeli, the fleshpots and their denizens are portrayed as a good deal more attractive than the narrow and bigoted asceticism which had accompanied success. Again, the moral is far from clear.

Contarini Fleming is much more evidently autobiographical. As has already been noted, the accounts of Contarini's schooldays are pretty clearly based on Disraeli's own experiences. So are the dislike of his mother, or stepmother in Contarini's case, and the loved, but distant, father. The latter is foreign minister in some mysterious Scandinavian state; and his son, by his own brilliance and audacity, se-

cures a dazzling diplomatic success which opens to him a
clear path to greatness. Here, however, Contarini is tripped
up by conflict within himself. Like Disraeli's other heroes,
he yearns for fame with a painful intensity, but he has
never been able to decide whether it should be as a statesman or an artist. Now, with fame as a statesman within his
grasp, his artistic nature rebels, and he pours forth his feelings in an anonymous novel. The authorship of the bitter
satire is discovered; and, reviled and his career ruined, Contarini flees into exile, giving Disraeli the opportunity to
conduct another guided tour, this time of the Mediterranean world. The conflict within Contarini is, however,
never completely resolved. At the end of the book we find
him, longing to be an artist, yet convinced that his will be
an active political career. Any reader who follows the balance of argument throughout the book would not be in
much doubt that this would be the conclusion. In the words
of Contarini's father:

> What were all the great poets of whom we now talk so
> much, what were they in their lifetime? The most miserable
> of their species. . . . A man of great energies aspires that
> they should be felt in his lifetime, that his existence should
> be rendered more intensely vital by the constant conscious-
> ness of his multiplied and multiplying power. . . . Would
> you rather have been Homer or Julius Caesar, Shakespeare or
> Napoleon? No one doubts. . . .

Disraeli certainly did not.

In Disraeli's case, however, the artist, or what passed for
one, played a role in the rise of the man of action. Lacking
blood, or a million, he at least had a genius, and his books
were part of the proof. It was they who introduced him to
Lytton Bulwer, and Lytton Bulwer who introduced him to
society. One of his first acts upon returning to England had
been to withdraw his name from the rolls of Lincoln's Inn.
By the middle of February 1832 he was "most comfortably
located in Duke Street," and happily launched into the

Mayfair swim. From there it was not far to politics, for several of the bright young dandies of Bulwer's and Disraeli's circle were also keen politicians, of the liberal Whig or Radical persuasion. Bulwer himself had been elected M.P. for St. Ives, Hunts., in 1831, and Disraeli was not long in attempting to follow his friend's example, if not quite his friend's politics.

TWO

Political Ambitions

THERE IS NO REASON whatever to believe that Disraeli would have had any objection to entering Parliament under the Whig aegis. He had, after all, ridiculed all parties, Tories and Radicals as well as Whigs, without favoritism. And the introduction of the Whig Reform Bill early in 1831, word of which had reached him in Constantinople, he had hailed as "wonderful news which . . . has quite unsettled my mind." Moreover, early in 1832 he was pretty clearly fishing for government support. He was, it is true, at the same time writing, or at least lending his name to, a violent diatribe against the government's foreign policy as being too pro-French. It was, as he said, a "John Bull book," to be published by Murray, with whom he had reestablished a business relationship, and was no more than a Tory tract, generously contributed to by Tory propagandists. As he himself admitted, it was "written by Legion," and though he cheerfully assumed the responsibility for them, there is no reason to suppose that the ideas expressed in it were his (not least because they ran dead against his later opinions).

Even if they had been, the book by itself would not have been sufficient to deprive him of government support had there been other good reason for it. For though, as he modestly put it, he would "destroy the foreign policy of the Grey faction," he proclaimed himself "still a Reformer"; and this gave Lord Grey's government an important claim on his support, and him a claim on theirs. What is more, he believed, and clearly hoped, that the minister with special responsibility for the Reform Bill, Lord John Russell, took a particular interest in his progress.

Disraeli greatly overrated this interest, if in fact it actually existed. Even if it had, it is unlikely that Russell or any other member of the government could have turned the trick for Disraeli in the only constituency where he had the slightest chance. Without money, and without claims on a powerful patron in government or elsewhere, Disraeli was surely right to turn his mind, as he did almost immediately on his return to England, to the borough of Wycombe. There he was at least known as a neighbor, which was some asset. It did not prove to be sufficient, for a variety of reasons.

Wycombe represented, in small compass, much of what the Reform agitation was all about. The power of election lay with the burgesses, the equivalent of freemen elsewhere. But late in the seventeenth century, the Corporation had assumed to itself the exclusive right to create new burgesses; and, as happened in many other places, this right was used to control elections. At first the existing burgesses were swamped by new creations. Then their numbers dwindled to an easily controllable, or so it was hoped, fifty or so. By Disraeli's time, and it had long been the case, the Corporation which passed for the town government, as well as the burgesses, was packed with political nominees, not a few of whom were nonresidents.

As elsewhere, this situation was bitterly resented by those who were excluded. Wycombe was a bustling little market and manufacturing town of some six thousand population, and it had grown prosperous during the past century on corn, lace, and paper (the chairmaking industry was just beginning). Exclusion was particularly, or at any rate most effectively, resented by a number of substantial men who felt that they had as good, and often a better, right to occupy the places of local honor and dignity than the members of the Corporation.

Thus far Wycombe's situation was not unlike that of a large number of other towns. But it had further characteristics, which, if by no means unique, were certainly not so generally shared. For the Corporation, though close, had never ended in anyone's pocket, and had never ceased to represent a variety of interests. Nor had it ever become completely unresponsive to popular pressure. The obstreperousness of both the Corporation and the mob, which had resulted among other things in his son being "taken to the town pump & pumped upon," had persuaded the first Marquis of Lansdowne* to give up around the turn of the century any attempt to dominate the town's politics. The Corporation had, however, continued to support Whig candidates. In 1831 the preference of the Corporation and the pressure of the populace had forced out Sir John Dashwood King, heir of the famous Sir Francis Dashwood of West Wycombe, because Dashwood King, who forty years before had helped to unseat the Lansdowne interest, now refused to support the Reform Bill. On that question Wycombe was virtually united, even the Tories feeling called upon to give at least nominal support to the cause.

Disraeli would have had little choice, therefore, but to stand as a Reformer. But, when a vacancy caused a by-election in June, he did not have the opportunity to stand as the candidate of the Reform government. The Whig majority in the Corporation had a much more eligible candidate for that honor, the Prime Minister's son. Disraeli was thus left with the possibilities of appealing to popular anti-Corporation feeling or to such Tory sentiment as existed. As it turned out, he was able to attract the latter by appealing to the former. He told Austen that he stood on

* Perhaps more famous as Lord Shelburne.

"the high Radical interest," and he took down with him the endorsement of prominent Radicals, such as Daniel O'Connell, Joseph Hume, and Sir Francis Burdett. In fact, none of them knew much about him. Nor did it become very apparent at Wycombe in precisely what sense he was a Radical. He talked a great deal about his solicitude for the people, and prided himself on having sprung from them and having no Plantagenet blood in his veins, but he had no specific proposals to advance. Though no friendly critic, the comment of the *Bucks Gazette* is a fair one. His principal supporters, the paper said, "were the radical party, who, though he did not, even in his professions, go beyond Col. Grey in liberality, in any one particular, nevertheless preferred him to one whom they viewed as a member of the aristocracy. . . . Mr. D'Israeli was also supported by the Tories. They, no doubt, see ample reason why they should avoid the Colonel, and prefer a young man of no political character, but very vaguely pledged," and who was willing to employ, as the *Gazette* went on to point out, the Tory agent in Wycombe as his own.

There is no reason to doubt that Disraeli's candidacy was genuinely popular at Wycombe. For, despite the vagueness of his principles and the extravagance of his appearance, his "curls and ruffles," and language, the young orator who harangued the populace from beside a red lion on an inn portico fulfilled a genuine need. To support him was to demonstrate opposition to the deeply resented privilege of the Corporation, and beyond that to the aristocratic privilege in which close corporations were rightly thought to play a part. The desire to be independent, to be one's own man and under no one's thumb, was strong at Wycombe, where it would long continue to be an important factor in town politics — and elsewhere. Disraeli's candidacy gave expression to that feeling. And because the Corporation he opposed happened to be Whig, and because he was willing to have Tory support, it is not difficult either to see why the latter party supported him. The mistake would be to see the two phenomena as having a connected importance and significance for Disraeli's future career. The coincidence is not portentous of Disraeli's later "Tory Democracy," nor, though he was undoubtedly familiar with Bolingbroke (he quoted him in *Vivian Grey*), was he yet putting his strategy to work. Disraeli was presenting himself as a Radical pure and simple, not yet as an aristocratic champion of the people.

In any case, his tactics did not secure him success. Though the Reform Act had already received the royal assent when the election took place, it was held under the old franchise; and true to form the burgesses voted twenty-three to twelve in Grey's favor. Disraeli had, however, established himself as a candidate and prepared the ground for the general election which was bound to follow soon. That would take place under the new franchise, and Disraeli could hope to have many more supporters among the £10 householders* in whom in Wycombe and all other boroughs the franchise was now to be vested.

Disraeli issued his address from Bradenham on 1 October 1832. It commenced with some rude remarks about a candidate who was private secretary to the First Lord of the Treasury, as Colonel Grey was to his father. It mentioned that the neighboring borough of Aylesbury had just escaped having the private secretary to the Lord Chancellor (Denis Le Marchant), and that he had been replaced by "an unknown youth, whose only recommendation is that he is the very young brother of a very inexperienced minister" (T. B. Hobhouse). All this was preliminary to his own qualifications. He was no mere government nominee, and opposed the "system of factious and intrusive nomination. . . ." He wore "the badge of no party, and the livery of no faction," but rather came forward as "an Independent neighbor." But, he said, and one suspects that he had in mind previous criticism, he would not use his "independ-

---

* Those who lived in a house with a rental value of £10 a year.

ence" as an excuse to avoid stating his opinions. He followed with nine points. He was for the secret ballot. He
was for triennial Parliaments, which, he contended, was the
old English way before the Whigs had deprived the country of them early in the eighteenth century. He advocated
the repeal of the so-called taxes on knowledge, taxes on
newspapers and on paper itself. So much was pure Radicalism, and so presumably was his rather unspecific reference
to "some great measure to ameliorate the condition of the
lower orders," and his pledge not to support any government which did not bring such a measure forward. His demand for the modification of the criminal code spoke to an
issue fashionable in all parties. So was economy and re-
trenchment. He waffled on the question of the abolition of
slavery, a touchy question in a county where the leader of
the Tory party, Lord Chandos, was also the national spokesman for the West Indian interest. And on two other highly
delicate questions he managed to be even more ambivalent.
On the Corn Laws,* he would "support any change the
basis of which is to relieve the customer without injuring
the farmer; and for the Church I am desirous of seeing ef-
fected some commutation which while it prevents the tithe
from acting as a tax on industry and enterprise, will again
render the clergy what I am always desirous of seeing them,
fairly remunerated, because they are valuable and efficient
labourers, and influential, because they are beloved."

Disraeli had remarked to Austen during his earlier
canvass: "Whigs, Tories, and Radicals, Quakers, Evangeli-
cals, Abolition of Slavery, Reform, Conservatism, Corn-
laws — here is hard work for one who is to please all
parties." His address was a noble effort to that end. His first
two points especially were the pure milk of Radicalism.
But there is much more interest in some aspects commented upon by the *Bucks Gazette*. The *Gazette* rightly
remarked that the new Tory *Bucks Herald* supported Disraeli "as earnestly as if they thought him a thorough going

---

* Protective duties which will be discussed in more detail later.

Tory," and the *Gazette* went on to say that on the issues of slavery, the Corn Laws, and the Church, it thought he was a Tory. Certainly on these issues — which happened to be the critical ones in Bucks — there was nothing in his stand to offend the Marquis of Chandos. He became more Tory as the campaign progressed, and he now begins to invoke the great Tory leaders of the previous century, pointing out that in advocating such measures as triennial Parliaments, which had been part of the stock in trade of the Tory opposition to Walpole, he was not ashamed to be "as great and as destructive a Radical as Sir William Wyndham and my Lord Bolingbroke."

Such arguments, however, did not sufficiently move even the new electors of Wycombe. The new franchise probably did not sweep low enough to draw in all of Disraeli's potential Radical support. In any case, before the election took place the Corporation had begun to make highly conciliatory gestures toward the excluded and to reform itself, which undoubtedly weakened the Radical cause. And, though the extension of the borough's boundaries brought in some Tory voters, there were still not enough of them. Disraeli was at the bottom of the poll, led by two Whigs.

Disraeli angrily charged of the Whigs that "the secret of their enmity was that he was not nobly born." He had, however, had almost enough of playing the gamin in his native county, and on the same day he was beaten at Wycombe, he issued an address to the electors of the county: "I come forward as the supporter of that great interest which is the only solid basis of the social fabric, and, convinced that the sound prosperity of this country depends upon the protected industry of the farmer, I would resist that spirit of rash and experimental legislation which is fast hurrying this once glorious Empire to the agony of civil convulsion." It hardly needs to be emphasized that these were rather strange sentiments for a Radical, particularly one who had intimated relief to the consumers of corn in Wycombe. Nor, of course, in attempting to join Chandos, the heir to the dukedom of Buckingham, as a county candidate was he exactly throwing in his lot with the poor and oppressed. Chandos, who was opposed by two Reformers (or Whigs), was not anxious to share the Tory cause or his position as the "Farmers' Friend" with anyone. But Disraeli's desire to do so had been anticipated by Charles Scott Murray, backed by strong public sentiment. Disraeli cheerfully gave way in his favor, arriving at the hustings in the carriage of the second Tory candidate.

Yet the country Disraeli and the city Disraeli were not the same, as was soon made evident. In April 1833 a vacancy occurred for Marylebone, and in the heady environment of the metropolis, Disraeli speedily shed his concern for a stable social fabric founded on Church and Land. He now came forward as one "supported by neither of the aristocratic parties," but as an "independent member of society who has no interest either direct or indirect, in corruption or misgovernment, and as one of a family untainted by the receipt of public money." He appealed for the votes of the Marylebone electors "as a man who has already fought the battle of the people. . . ." The points that followed were pure Radicalism, without the Wycombe adulterations. Disraeli had quoted to Sarah an imaginary exchange printed in the *Town,* in which the new candidate had been asked on what he intended to stand. "On my head" was the answer — not far wrong.

Shortly thereafter Disraeli essayed what purported to be a serious answer to what was certainly a serious question — *What is He?* The pamphlet started with the proposition that the first object of every statesman is strong government. By what means and on what principles was this to be achieved? Disraeli contended that "we must either revert to the *aristocratic* principle, or we must advance to the *democratic.* . . ." The aristocratic principle of government was, he said, since the passage of the Reform Act, dead. It therefore became "the duty of every person of property, talents, and education, unconnected with the unhappy party at present in power, to use his utmost exertions to advance the democratic principle. . . ." "A Tory and a Radical," he went on, "I understand; a Whig — a democratic aristocrat, I cannot comprehend. If the Tories indeed despair of restoring the aristocratic principle, and are sincere in their avowal that the State cannot be governed with the present machinery, it is their duty to coalesce with the Radicals, and permit both political nicknames to merge in the common, the intelligible, and the dignified title of a National Party." That all this was intelligible may perhaps be open to question. For the prescription which was to bring it about was triennial Parliaments, the ballot, and an immediate dissolution. The result presumably would have been the return of people of "property, talents, and education." But, as the Whigs prided themselves on precisely these same qualities, the operative phrase was clearly "unconnected with the unhappy party at present in power." It was utter nonsense. Monypenny, who contends that far from showing a man without political convictions, Disraeli's first year in politics shows a man overburdened with them, finds the interesting point that even in this early period "all the elements of his finished political creed can already be detected." One can indeed find all those elements — and a good many more — but in no discernible relationship to one another.

Meanwhile, Disraeli's private and professional lives were full of activity, and by no means all of his energies were absorbed in politics. He had become an author of some reputation, and, in so far as he earned his bread, it was by writing. But he had other demanding pursuits. In 1832, not long after his return from abroad, he acquired what appears to have been his first full-fledged mistress. Clara Bolton was the wife of a fashionable doctor who had treated Disraeli's earlier illnesses. She gave him the mothering he required, but she does not emerge as a pleasant personality. This may, however, have something to do with the fact that the main part she plays in Disraeli's life is as the mistress of the husband of his next mistress, and not very satisfied with her part of the bargain.

Sometime in the spring of 1833 Disraeli made the acquaintance of Henrietta, the wife of Sir Francis Sykes. She was approximately his own age, young, beautiful, and highly sexed. By, the summer they were in the midst of a passionate affair. She paid a visit to Bradenham. He returned with her to Southend, where she and her husband had taken a house. Clearly Sir Francis was not an overly watchful spouse, for in August, when Disraeli had returned to Bradenham, Henrietta writes to him at midnight that "it is the night Dearest the night that we used to pass so happily together." "The dear head is it better? That it were pillowed on my bosom for ever." And she signs herself — "your Mother." Evidently she was more than that.

Sir Francis was busy with Mrs. Bolton. But she appears to have incited him to umbrage at being cuckolded by her former lover. Henrietta had returned to London, and there Sir Francis descended upon her and made a scene. His wife, suspecting the evil influence of Mrs. Bolton, decided to pay a call and confront her enemy. As luck would have it, she also found Sir Francis, and, walking in unannounced, poured out her wrath on both. She also used the occasion of this undoubted victory to secure an agreement for a maintenance of the status quo.

The husband was now temporarily neutralized. But the affair became well known, and Henrietta's father, a wealthy brewer from Norfolk, was scandalized. Meeting his daughter and her lover on the street in London, he demonstrated his disapproval by ostentatiously cutting them. Unfortunately for him, his ostentation was lost on them, for so engrossed were they with each other that they failed to notice him! So he was reduced to the rather unsatisfactory expedient of informing them through a third party that they had been cut, and would be until their relationship ended.

Their relationship was far from ending. It went on in the same way in London and in the country, where they continued to take holidays together, often in company with Sir Francis, and sometimes joined by the Boltons! Henrietta gave him the female admiration he found so necessary. And, with her as his muse, by the autumn he was at work on an epic poem and a novel. The terrible craving for greatness had not left him, and he had decided to pursue it now by turning his hand to poetry. The idea had come to him, he said, standing on the plains of Troy and musing on great epics from Homer onward. The *Iliad* had been the great heroic epic, the *Aeneid* the great political epic, while Dante had excelled with a national epic. Then it struck him. " 'What!' I exclaimed, 'is the revolution of France a less important event than the siege of Troy? Is Napoleon a less interesting character than Achilles? For me remains the Revolutionary Epick.' "

The work is mainly interesting as a celebration of revolution by the future leader of the Conservative party, and as again revealing what was to be a continuing fascination with Napoleon. He dreamed of himself as a hero on the same proportions. Unfortunately, the poem did not make him so. It first came before the public at the Austens'. They, who had become little more to Disraeli than a source of loans, rightly felt neglected. To appease them, he agreed to come to dinner, bring a canto of his poem, and allow Mrs. Austen to take the credit for introducing the new literary lion, at any rate in his poetic form, to the world. The Austens' nephew, later the famous excavator of Nineveh and a diplomat, Sir Henry Layard, remembered that

> there was something irresistibly comic in the young man dressed in the fantastic, coxcombical costume that he then affected — velvet coat of an original cut thrown wide open, and ruffles to its sleeves, shirt collars turned down in Byronic fashion, an elaborately embroidered waistcoat whence issued voluminous folds of frill, and shoes adorned with red rosettes — his black hair pomatumed and elaborately curled, and his person redolent with perfume — announcing himself as the Homer or Dante of the age.

That he was not, and though he published what he had written, in March and June 1834, the reception did not encourage him to finish the work.

By then, however, Disraeli's social life at least was prospering. In April Sir Francis took himself off on a tour of the Continent, and Disraeli virtually moved in with Henrietta in Upper Grosvenor Street. Together they did the London season. They were not, certainly, entertained by the most exclusive hostesses, but by those, like Henrietta herself, who had a slightly raffish reputation. But such hostesses were still popular with the greatest and most powerful, some of whom were more than a little disreputable themselves. It is generally supposed that it was during this season that Sheridan's daughter and Melbourne's unfortunate friend, Mrs. Norton, introduced Disraeli to the future Premier, giving rise to the famous exchange: "Well now, tell me what do you want to be?" asked Melbourne. "I want to be Prime Minister."

It was certainly during this season, at a dinner party given by Henrietta herself on 10 July, that Disraeli met the man who more than any other perhaps was to put him on the path to that office. The American portrait painter John Singleton Copley fled radical Boston in 1774 for the more congenial society of Europe, first of Rome, then of London. He was accompanied by his young son of the same name, and the latter ultimately rose to eminence at the Bar and in politics. One of his great assets in the latter sphere was the well-known flexibility of his principles. Thus in 1827, when the "Catholic" (i.e., pro-Emancipation) Canning was searching desperately for some "Protestant" members for his new government, Copley, who had been Master of the Rolls in the previous government, accommodated and was rewarded by being made Baron Lyndhurst and Lord Chancellor. He retained that office in the Goderich ministry that followed, and, having served to undermine Goderich, continued in that role in the succeeding Wellington government. It was the Duke's inflexibility, not Lyndhurst's, that

broke that government, and the latter cheerfully accepted
a judicial plum offered him by the Whigs. Lyndhurst felt it
unnecessary, however, to repay the gift with political gratitude, and indulged in intrigue and opposition whenever
he felt moved to do so. In the summer of 1834 he was high
in the councils of Peel's reviving Conservative party, and
was soon to resume his old seat on the Woolsack.

Lyndhurst was also a man with a powerful sex drive. He
was strongly attracted to Henrietta, and there can be little
doubt that his passion was gratified. They soon traveled
openly together, later even visiting Bradenham, to the
scandal of Buckinghamshire society. At first, probably
partly to please Henrietta, Lyndhurst took an interest in
her young friend. But the relationship grew and blossomed.
Doubtless the older man saw in the younger a kindred
spirit — another supreme cynic. Certainly there is nothing
in their long friendship that would dispel such an assumption.

In the late spring and summer of 1834 the great Reform
ministry was tottering toward its final dissolution. In July,
Lord Grey, feeling betrayed by his colleagues in his Irish
policy, at last implemented his frequent threats to resign.
Melbourne, with many of his old colleagues, took Grey's
place. But in November he was dismissed by William IV,
who sensed a growing radicalism in the ministry and its
supporters. Peel was in Italy, but Wellington, and the inevitable Lyndhurst, stepped in and filled the gap until his
return.

During these unsettled times Disraeli was madly maneuvering for political support, any kind of political support.
In June, at the house of another of his regular hostesses,
Lady Blessington, the lover of the famous dandy the Count
D'Orsay, he met the great hope of the Radicals, Lord Durham, and spent the whole evening in deep conversation.
This was, it is true, before he met Lyndhurst; but Disraeli
was not the man to abandon one string to his bow just because he had found a second. On 17 November he wrote

asking for Durham's intervention in his behalf at Aylesbury. But on 28 November he wrote to Sarah that Wellington and Lyndhurst were doing their best for him at Wycombe, pressing the first Lord Carrington, who unlike his
son was a Tory, to support him. Lyndhurst was also doing
his best elsewhere. On 6 December the diarist Greville records:

> The Chancellor called on me yesterday about getting young
> Disraeli into Parliament (through the means of George Ben-
> tinck) for Lynn. I told him George wanted a good man to as-
> sist in turning out William Lennox, and he suggested the
> above-named gentleman, whom he called a friend of Chandos.
> His political principles must, however, be in abeyance, for
> he said that Durham was doing all he could to get him by the
> offer of a seat, and so forth; if therefore he is undecided and
> wavering between Chandos and Durham, he must be a mighty
> impartial personage. I don't think such a man will do, though
> just such as Lyndhurst would be connected with.

In the end, Disraeli settled once more for Wycombe, this
time supported by £500 from Wellington's campaign fund.
His election battle is mainly notable for a long speech he
delivered on 16 December and subsequently published as a
pamphlet entitled *The Crisis Examined.* The most remark
able thing about the speech is the startling coincidence between the views expressed in it and those contained in the
Tamworth Manifesto, the draft of which Peel read to the
Cabinet on the same evening. Indeed it is too startling to
have been merely the happy coincidence, Disraeli and the
party he was about to join reaching the same position of
progressive Conservatism at the same time, that Monypenny imagined. And, though Disraeli could obviously not
have seen the actual draft, its main outlines had been discussed at least as early as the Cabinet of 11 December, making it more than probable that he would have known of the
gist of it through Lyndhurst. The main points of his speech
are identical with those of the Manifesto; the expression of
reverence for the established institutions of the country, but

the endorsement of Church reform, municipal reform, and the need to settle Dissenting grievances. He also threw in his endorsement of Chandos's pet scheme for the abolition of the Malt Tax, subsequently appearing at Aylesbury to give the Marquis his vocal support. Once again, however, all his politicking was for present purposes in vain. The Tory leaders had not been able to secure Lord Carrington's interest, which remained as it had long been at the disposal of his eldest son, the Whiggish Robert John Smith, himself a candidate. That interest might well have done Disraeli some good, but without it he finished at the bottom of the poll, behind his two Whig opponents.

Thus he was forced to report to the Duke of Wellington that "I have fought *our* battle and I have lost it. . . ." Throughout the election there had never been much need to take seriously his protests of continuing independence; and a few weeks later, at his own request, he was put up for that citadel of Toryism, the Carlton Club. He was proposed by Lord Strangford and seconded by Chandos, neither exactly a paladin of Peel's progressive new Conservatism. But consistency had never been Disraeli's strong suit, and, though he might not yet have found his exact place within it, he had at least, after much wandering, found a party at last.

For the next couple of years Disraeli's public energies were to be almost exclusively devoted to politics and to political writing. He settled in, in effect, as Lyndhurst's private secretary. He did good service, and he enjoyed the great man's continuing support. Unfortunately, Lyndhurst was not in office, as the general election had gone against the government. He did his best, however, to advance Disraeli's political career. In April 1835 the latter was sent down with the party's blessing to contest a by-election at Taunton. It was the first occasion on which he began squarely to tackle the problem of blending his past Radicalism with his present Toryism, emerging in the central thesis, much elaborated later, that "the Conservative party

was the really democratic party in the country who surrounded the people with the power of the Throne to shield
them from the undue power of the aristocracy. . . ." Of
this, more later.

The other main consequence of the contest, which as
usual he lost, was to be a famous exchange with Daniel
O'Connell which ended in Disraeli's challenging him to
duel. Disraeli had had some strong things to say about
O'Connell's encouragement of violence in Ireland. O'Connell, who had not forgotten Disraeli's earlier request for an
endorsement, replied with a bitter attack on his lack of
political consistency, in which he said among other things
that Disraeli was one of the worst of his race. "He has just
the qualities of the impenitent thief on the Cross, and I
verily believe, if Mr. Disraeli's family herald were to be examined and his genealogy traced, the same personage would
be discovered to be the heir at law of the exalted individual to whom I allude." Disraeli not entirely surprisingly
took violent exception to these remarks, and replied with a
challenge. O'Connell, who had once killed a man in a duel,
declined, as he always did. Disraeli then turned to O'Connell's son, Morgan, to defend his father's honor. Morgan
replied that he would not hold himself responsible for all
his father's remarks, and that it was not his father who had
been insulted. Disraeli responded with a letter to the newspapers which more than made up for any omission in that
respect. But at this point the authorities intervened, and
the affair ended without violence, though with much notoriety for Disraeli.

Disraeli threw himself heart and soul into the schemes
and plans of his noble patron. In a memorandum written
in 1836 Disraeli said that in the autumn of 1834, before the
Whig government had fallen, Lyndhurst "was looking
about for a party to put in motion which might not seem
factious." The result was their cooperation with Chandos
in launching the movement against the Malt Tax, a move-

ment that was to cause Peel's government, which had no intention of repealing it, considerable embarrassment. This was certainly not their object, but Lyndhurst continued to cast about in ways which often caused difficulties and embarrassments for his chief. In the autumn of 1835, when Peel had deliberately exercised restraint in opposing the second Melbourne government's Municipal Corporations Bill in the House of Commons, Lyndhurst led an intense opposition in the Lords, which succeeded in eliminating from the measure some of its more liberal and democratic features. Disraeli was hand in glove with his patron, which was strange work for the one-time opponent of the Wycombe Corporation (the bill was aimed at throwing open the old close corporations and establishing some uniform and responsible government in their places), and for the late champion of democratic Toryism.

Not that Disraeli had ceased to be the champion of democratic Toryism. Indeed, he chose to elaborate the theory further in a two-hundred-page pamphlet, published in large part to vindicate Lyndhurst and the Lords for their opposition to this very bill! In the *Vindication of the English Constitution* published in 1835 and the *Letters of Runnymede* published in 1836, Disraeli advances most of the arguments later taken further in the trilogy. He contends that since the seventeenth century, when the Whigs emasculated the monarchy and established themselves as a close aristocratic oligarchy, the Tories had been the real champions of the nation and the people. He cites the popular rhetoric of Bolingbroke in opposition, and claims that this comes to fruition in the policies of the younger Pitt. He gives the recent examples of the Chandos clause, which enfranchised the tenant farmers, and Lyndhurst's defense of the freeman franchise during the passage of the Reform Act. He charges that the Reform Act itself was partial and undemocratic, merely shifting power to middle-class Dissenters and others likely to be favorable to the Whigs. In the *Letters of Runnymede,* or more accurately "The Spirit of Whiggism,"* is one of the dramatic quotes to which Disraeli could hearken back in 1867:

> The disposition of property in England throws the government of the country into the hands of its natural aristocracy. I do not believe that any scheme of the suffrage, or any method of election, could divert that power into other quarters. It is the necessary consequence of our present social state. I believe, the wider the popular suffrage, the more powerful would be the natural aristocracy. This seems to me an inevitable consequence; but I admit this proposition on the clear understanding that such an extension should be established upon a fair, and not a factious, basis.

We shall look more closely at Disraeli's theories later. For the moment it is only necessary to remark that, however well this might look in 1867 and later, it does not always accord very well with Disraeli's practice before that date. And though his theories are now taking on a certain consistency (as always, there is a great deal of nonsense mixed in), one must not suppose that he always, or even usually, attempted to practice what he preached.

Yet, whatever the merits of Disraeli's thought and actions, there can be no doubt that he was useful to the party; and he was on the eve of getting his reward. He was also about to emerge from a tumultuous and hectic private life into the domestic bliss which he was to enjoy for almost three decades. For in the autumn of 1836 the affair with Henrietta finally ended. It had gone on with a fair amount of passion until then. There had been signs almost from the beginning, however, that Disraeli was not entirely comfortable with the situation. Indeed, it is very likely that for most of the time he had been more in love with love, with a romantic drama required of all Byronic heroes, than with Henrietta. What he craved was a comfortable, stable,

---

* An essay published with the "Letters," which were a series of bitter invectives on enemies and puffs of Conservative leaders that had appeared in *The Times.*

loving environment into which to flee the cares and abuse of the world. Henrietta was too passionate, too demanding, and probably too highly sexed to provide what he sought. Her simultaneous affair with Lyndhurst had not bothered him, but the late 1837 liaison with the painter Daniel Maclise was to provide the occasion for the final breach. Though it did not happen without causing a wrench, it was not long before Disraeli was heaving great sighs of relief. Better times were just around the corner.

THREE

The Climb to Leadership

ON 20 JUNE 1837, William IV, the last of George III's sons to sit upon the British throne, died. Disraeli rode in Lyndhurst's carriage to Kensington Palace, where the former Lord Chancellor attended the Privy Council, "and kissed the young Queen's hand, which all agreed was remarkably sweet and soft." Victoria's reign, in which Disraeli was to play so prominent a role, had begun.

It began auspiciously for Disraeli. At that time a monarch's death was automatically followed by a dissolution of Parliament. In the subsequent canvassing, the Maidstone Conservatives decided that they were strong enough to put forward a second candidate. They sent to the Carlton for one, and the choice fell on Disraeli. "The clouds have at length dispelled," he wrote joyfully to Sarah on 30 June, "and my prospects seem as bright as day." This time he was not to be disappointed; the two Conservatives won handsomely.

The summer and autumn passed in the new member visiting and being visited, and on 15 November he took his seat. As luck would have it, almost the first item of business after the opening formalities was a vote on Jewish disabilities. The Sheriffs of London, one of whom, much to Disraeli's amusement, was a Sir Moses, presented petitions. "Nobody looked at me, and I was not at all uncomfortable, but voted in the majority with the utmost *sangfroid. . . .*" The majority was against the Jewish cause. It is true that the main question was a bill to relieve Quakers and Moravians, and that the Jewish question had been added by an amendment. It is also true that the liberal promoters of the bill, though favorable to the Jewish cause, opposed the amendment as impolitic and diversionary. But this was not the reason why those on Disraeli's side of the House voted against it, for they were opposed to all such relief, whether for Protestant nonconformists or for Jews. Clearly Disraeli was not desirous of disassociating himself with such opinion. For a new member, particularly one who had been taunted at his own election with cries of "old clothes" and "Shylock," his action is probably understandable. But the incident underlines one of the disadvantages he labored under, more especially in his own party, from the beginning of his parliamentary life.

He was not long to remain reticent, however. The Jewish vote came on 5 December. On the evening of the seventh he rose to deliver his maiden speech. The speech he had prepared could only have brought immense derision on his head. It was hopelessly affected, full of convoluted sentences and impossible images. Fortunately the subject he had chosen assured that no one heard it. He intended to attack O'Connell and his party for practicing violence and coercion in the Irish elections. But hardly had he commenced than the hooting and laughter of the Irish members began to drown him out. The longer he continued, the louder became the din. He remained on his feet for the full time he had allotted himself, but for most of the time his speech was no more than mute mouthing to the rest of the House. The great exception was the thunderous final sentence, which all agreed rose high above the clamor: "I sit down now, but the time will come when you will hear me."

Actually, the time came very quickly. His adversaries had not only saved him from an egregious failure, they had also, by persecuting him, won him considerable sympathy. And he was treated to good advice, oddly enough by an Irish M.P., Richard Sheil, who advised him to "get rid of your genius for a session. Speak often, for you must not show yourself cowed, but speak shortly. Be very quiet, try to be dull, only argue and reason imperfectly, for if you reason with precision, they will think you are trying to be witty. Astonish them by speaking on subjects of detail. Quote figures, dates, calculations. And in a short time the House will sigh for the wit and eloquence which they all know are in you. . . ." Ten days after the initial debacle, Disraeli acted on this advice, delivering himself on a subject in which he was an expert, the law of copyright. He did not attempt a formal speech, and his remarks were mainly highly technical. But the results were all he could have wished. He was heard "with the utmost curiosity and attention," and "sat down with a general cheer." He spoke again in March in defense of the Corn Laws, and reported to his sister that "in the lobby, all the squires came up to shake hands with me, and thank me for the good service. They were so grateful, and well they might be, for certainly they had nothing to say for themselves." Evidently he was not filled with admiration for the men who constituted the backbone of his party in Parliament. Finally, with characteristic defiance, he closed his speaking for the session with another speech on Ireland. This time he was pleased that he spoke "with spirit and success. I thought it well that my voice should be heard at the end of the session, and especially on an Irish subject." Disraeli had found his feet.

Hardly had he achieved his first parliamentary successes than he was also launched on the path toward a supremely happy marriage. In March 1838 Wyndham Lewis, Disraeli's colleague at Maidstone, who had also generously borne most of the expenses involved in the election, died. Disraeli at once set about comforting the grieving widow, and by

December the language of passion had replaced that of solace. His first hero, Vivian Grey, had "looked upon marriage as a comedy in which, sooner or later, he was as a well-paid actor to play his part. . . . But of all the wives in the world, a young and handsome one was that which he most dreaded; and how a statesman who was wedded to a beautiful woman could possibly perform his duties to the public, did most exceedingly puzzle him." Mrs. Wyndham Lewis fitted this prescription, or seemed to, almost exactly. She was the widow of a rich man, at forty-four she was twelve years Disraeli's senior, and, though far from ugly, the blush of youthful beauty was obviously gone. Certainly he had hardly been swept off his feet at their first meeting at Bulwer Lytton's in 1832: "I was introduced, 'by particular desire,' to Mrs. Wyndham Lewis, a pretty little woman, a flirt, and a rattle; indeed gifted with a volubility I should think unequalled, and of which I can convey no idea. She told me that she liked 'silent, melancholy men.' I answered that I had no doubt of it."

In February 1839, when an already well advanced courtship was interrupted by her suspicions about his motives, he wrote remarkably frankly about them:

> I avow, when I first made my advances to you, I was influenced by no romantic feelings. My father had long wished me to marry; my settling in life was the implied, though not stipulated, condition of a disposition of his property, which would have been convenient to me. I myself about to commence a practical career, wished for the solace of a home, and shrunk from all the torturing passions of intrigue. I was not blind to worldly advantages in such an alliance. . . . [But] I found you in sorrow, and [my] heart was touched. I found you, as I thought, amiable tender, and yet acute and gifted with no ordinary mind, — one whom I could look upon with pride as the partner of my life, who could sympathize with all my projects and feelings, console me in the moments of depression, share my hour of triumph, and work with me for our honor and happiness.
>
> Now for your fortune: I write the sheer truth. That fortune proved to be much less than I, or the world, imagined. It was

in fact, as far as I was concerned, a fortune which could not
benefit me in the slightest degree. . . .

That was going much too far. Though she was not the heir
to her husband's large Welsh mining and ironmaking fortune, an income of £4,000 a year and a fine house in Grosvenor Gate (now 29 Park Lane) were hardly of no use to a
young M.P. with no certain income, and with what had
now become immense debts.

Still Disraeli was undoubtedly justified in claiming that
he would never have married for money alone. As he told
his future wife, he did sincerely desire to please his adored
father. He had written to her not long after Wyndham
Lewis's death that "the first wish of my life has ever been
that after all his kindness to me, and all the anxiety I have
cost him, he should live to see me settled and steady, and
successful to his heart's content." There surely was the
genuine voice of an eldest son. And his heart yearned for a
home of his own, the home an aging parent could not long
promise. Once again to his future wife he wrote from
Bradenham:

> I leave this place with great regret, even tho' the sun do not
> shine. After a week or so, one gets used to quiet habits, and
> feels, as I always do, the charm of domestic bliss. I experience
> a reluctance in once more entering the scene of strife and
> struggle, but after all, like the shower bath, it needs only a
> plunge. I never leave home without feeling as I did when I
> went to school, which is an odd though true thing for one to
> say who has been such a wanderer. A return, however, makes
> me just as nervous. I dread to detect the progress of time, and
> always anticipate misfortune.

It is a glimpse behind the brazen mask he presented to the
world.

Yet the basic reality of the man, though like most of us
he probably would never have fully recognized the fundamental truths about himself, was his immense egotism and
ambition. As he had said in different words to his sister

Sarah, so he now said to his intended, he desperately needed someone "who could sympathise with all my projects and feelings, console me in the moments of depression, share my hour of triumph," someone, in short, who could support the statesman in performing his duties to the public — and to himself.

It is not strange that he found Mary Anne Lewis, in the words of the glowing tribute he later paid her, "a perfect wife." Her confidence in him and admiration were complete, and scarcely had he been returned for Maidstone, much less taken his seat, than she was predicting to her brother, "Mark what I say — mark what I prophesy: Mr. Disraeli will in a very few years be one of the greatest men of his day." It is hardly surprising Disraeli found her acute! But she undoubtedly had considerable ability, particularly in the areas where Disraeli was most lacking. She came from solid yeoman stock in Devon, and, though like many families, hers could boast of "relations," her father was an impecunious naval lieutenant who died young. Doubtless she had early learned to be a shrewd manager. She certainly was as Disraeli's wife (much to the chagrin of the Wycombe shopkeepers). And not only did she manage well on what she had, she even set about paying off her husband's debts, and might have succeeded had he been entirely frank with her. Completely devoted to him, she was ready to lift from his shoulders all the details of life, to be nurse and mother, and to leave him unimpeded in the pursuit of his career.

In some ways, perhaps, she was not an asset. As Disraeli himself had early noticed, she was garrulous in the extreme. And the stories of her gaucheries are myriad, among the more delightful being her remark to some ladies who were engaged in a discussion of the beauties of Greek statues, "Oh, but you ought to see my Dizzy in his bath!" Or her breakfast table comment to the famous general Lord Hardinge after she and her husband had spent the night in the room next to his: "Oh, Lord Hardinge, I think I must be the happiest of women! When I woke up this morning, I said to myself: 'How lucky I am! I've been sleeping between the greatest orator and the greatest soldier of the day!' " Even her husband passed on a story of her small talk, apparently mildly erotic till the end. It was during her final illness, but she had rallied sufficiently to accompany him to an evening party. As Disraeli recounted it, she delighted her host, the future Lord Carlingford, "by telling him that she had heard him very much praised. He pressed her very much when and where. She replied 'It was in bed.' " Disraeli was surely right when he said of her (to Gladstone, who was very fond of Mary Anne, if not of her husband) that she was a "vivid and original character." A more conventional husband might have been harmed by her peculiarities. But Disraeli was not a conventional man. The complete loyalty and devotion she gave were all that he asked. Whether he took private note of her oddities it is impossible to say; but it is certain that no one else did, at any rate more than once, in his presence. And there is no evidence that to him she was ever any less than "a perfect wife."

They were married on 28 August 1839, the day after Parliament was prorogued, at St. George's, Hanover Square; and a long honeymoon, consisting of a German tour and a stay in Paris, followed. Early in December they returned to Grosvenor Gate, and a new life began for Disraeli. One great change that marriage made was to end his most pressing financial difficulties, and they had been very pressing indeed. Previous to his marriage he had had no income but what he could derive from his pen or borrow from his father and others. The yield from his pen had not been very great since *The Young Duke*. Neither *Contarini Fleming* nor *Alroy*, though they added to his literary reputation, made any money. *The Revolutionary Epick* yielded no return in either respect. And his political pamphleteering and journalism, though they gained him the gratitude of his patron and his party, did nothing for his purse. It is true that *Henrietta Temple*, begun in the first flush of his romance with Henrietta Sykes but not published until after it ended, had been a financial success. It is not entirely easy to see why. According to Philip Guedalla's introduction in the Bradenham Edition, "the rustle of real petticoats is more audible than in any other part of Disraeli's work." Perhaps because we are no longer used to the rustle of petticoats, the authenticity of feeling is less evident today. There are certainly genuinely autobiographical passages. The assertion of the all-consuming nature of true love, written at a time when he was experiencing it, carries conviction. So does the description of the terrible moment when it dawns that the once idolized love has become an object of repugnance. Nor can anyone doubt that he believed it when he said that there were few great men behind whom there was not "the spirit and sympathy of woman," or that "a female friend, amiable, clever, and devoted, is a possession more valuable than parks and palaces; and, without such a muse, few men can succeed in life, none be content." Equally convincing, and somewhat jarring, is the savage caricature, complete with dialect, of the Jewish moneylender.

Doubtless he had suffered much from moneylenders, for it was mainly due to borrowing and reborrowing that by the time of his marriage his debts were close to £20,000. On such a sum, the modest profits of *Henrietta Temple,* and the even more modest profits of *Venetia,* published in 1837, made hardly a dent; and, without the generous infusions of Mary Anne's money, willingly pledged, it is difficult to see how he ever would have escaped from the morass of his debts. To his cost, he was too proud to let her completely into his confidence, and he continued to accumulate debts faster than he ought to have done. But never thereafter, at any rate, did he have to fear, as he frequently had in the past, being arrested for his debts; and his wife's income sufficed to keep them in comfort as well.

Perhaps the most interesting thing about *Venetia* (for there is not much to be said in its favor), which came out in May, is the fact that in it the man who the following month was to be elected Tory M.P. for Maidstone chose to celebrate two notorious opponents of the establishment in Church and State, Shelley and Byron. In fact, however, radicalism of a sort was to be a prominent part of the political stance of the new Tory member. There was no Radical party, and about all that Radicals had in common was a tendency to sympathize with popular causes — though not necessarily with the same popular causes. Most Radicals, like Shelley and Byron, would have been in the libertarian tradition, and most would have voted with the Whigs in a clinch. Neither characteristic, of course, was to be found in the Disraelian version of radicalism. But there were some Radicals, though very far from a majority, who shared in a growing popular revulsion against the prevailing doctrines of political economy and the tendency of those doctrines toward laissez-faire in all economic matters. Some, such as the great Unitarian manufacturer John Fielden, came from the libertarian tradition. But not a few came out of a strong Tory tradition. Not surprisingly, Disraeli kept close to the latter, though, as with many of his positions, he did not always bother to make the distinctions clear.

A common bugbear of this anti-laissez-faire school of radicalism was the New Poor Law of 1834. A Reformed Parliament, with a predominantly rate-paying electorate, was bound to do something about what their constituents felt was a crushing burden of rates. But what gave the New Poor Law its particular twist were the theories of the so-called Philosophical Radicals, who largely shaped the act. They believed, with Malthus, that, unrestrained, population always tended to outgrow the available resources, and thus progressively to pauperize itself. They also held with Malthus that the only solution to the problem was moral restraint. As disciples of Jeremy Bentham they had confidence in the possibility of social engineering, through the manipulation of the pleasure and pain principle. As applied to the New Poor Law, this meant that poor relief should be made as painful as possible, among other means, through deprivation of sex and a diet as repulsive as was compatible with continued existence. To make sure that these theories were applied, all paupers were henceforward to be herded into workhouses, where life was to be made in every respect less eligible than on the outside. The result, it was hoped, would be a population happy in abstention and hard work. Not very surprisingly, the result was massive discontent.

Some Tories of the more radical variety attempted to exploit this issue in the 1837 election. A leading part was taken by John Walter, the proprietor of *The Times,* who was also M.P. for Berkshire. The new Tory candidate for Maidstone was not far behind. He rightly claimed that as a Buckingham Justice of the Peace he knew the problem at first hand; and this would have been especially true of a J.P. resident near Wycombe, where there was strong discontent. He left no room for uncertainty about his opinions. The act erred egregiously, he said, in going on "the principle that relief to the poor is a *charity.* I maintain that it is a *right!*" He closed with ringing phrases: "To sum up my feelings in a sentence — I consider that this Act has disgraced the country more than any other upon record. Both a moral crime and a political blunder, it announces to the world that in England poverty is a crime."

It is doubtful that the issue did him much good at Maidstone. Walter lost in Berkshire; and, though in some places the cry may have been useful in mobilizing pressure on the electorate from the outside, it is unlikely that in most places it would have been very popular within it. Disraeli, however, acted up to his assertions. In 1839 he was among the tiny minority of thirteen, who, acting against the lead of both front benches (for the Peel of the Tamworth Manifesto was keenly sensitive to the prejudices of the rate-paying electorate), supported Fielden's motion for the immediate repeal of the New Poor Law.

Before the session was over Disraeli was to find himself in still stranger company. In the years 1838 and 1839 a variety of social, economic, and political discontents combined to produce the Chartist movement. Movement may be too strong a term, for there was perhaps more disparity than unity in Chartism. In part, it had its origins in that phenomenon we call the Industrial Revolution,* which inevitably produced immense dislocations and cruel grievances. One was the New Poor Law. Another was the plight of those mechanization had left, and was continuously leaving, behind. Yet, if machines deprived some people of work, they also lay behind the long hours of others, laboring so that their employer could get a return on his heavy capital investment. Such grievances produced bitterness and rancor, which was greatly exacerbated by the bad harvests and accompanying trade depression of the last years of the 1830s. The result was to combine all the discontents under one standard, not social or economic, but political. One reason, doubtless, was that in hard times strikes and other forms of economic pressure are unlikely to achieve much, making political forms of expression more attractive. But the other reason was that there was a genuine commitment among many of those excluded from the 1832 franchise to the civic and political equality embodied in the six points of the famous People's Charter: universal manhood suffrage, annual Parliaments, voting by ballot, equal electoral districts, no property qualifications for members of Parliament, and payment of members.

Like most members of Parliament, Disraeli did not treat that commitment seriously. Nor did he, in the debate on 12 July on whether the House should consider the petition for the Charter signed by a million and a half persons, advocate an extension of political rights. The difficulty, it was true, lay in the Reform Act of 1832 and the constitution which it had established. It had deprived the few of power,

* Though, in fact, it was a complex blend of demographic, agricultural, commercial, and attitudinal, as well as industrial, elements.

to vest it in a much larger, but still arbitrary and partial, constituency. The old constitution had assumed that the few would have not only power but responsibility for the welfare of the many, as for example in the J.P.'s administering the Poor Laws. But the new constituency wanted power without responsibility. As the New Poor Law proved, they repudiated social duties and, taking power away from the justices, vested it in an impersonal central government. This new constituency, what he portrayed as the new ruling class, was the source of all difficulties. The Chartists made no attack on the aristocracy, it was against government by the middle classes that they inveighed. And, however much he might disapprove of the Charter, Disraeli declared himself not ashamed to say that he sympathized with the Chartists. They represented a large and important body of his countrymen, and they labored under great grievances. Having made this protest against the indifference with which the petition was treated on both sides of the House, he ended by joining the majority of 235, to 46, that voted against considering the Charter.

Disraeli nonetheless continued to manifest his sympathy with the Chartists. By this time the center of Chartist activity had moved. The National Convention, which had met in London early in the year, had now transferred itself to Birmingham, where, partly in response to parliamentary indifference, violence and rioting occurred. Disraeli joined Fielden and another extreme Radical to make up the minority of three that opposed special assistance to the Birmingham Corporation without an inquiry into the broad causes of unrest. In 1840 he once again voted with tiny minorities attempting to secure mitigation of the sentences of the Chartist leaders.

How does one explain Disraeli's actions, which not surprisingly caused many to believe him much more extreme than he actually was, and which put him at odds with the leaders of his own party? Part of the reason was undoubtedly what he said it was, a genuine sympathy with the sufferings that lay behind the Chartist agitation. As *Sybil* was further to demonstrate, Disraeli had a perception of the problems of the working classes, and an understanding of the social and political implications of those problems, rare among his contemporaries. He overemphasized, and knew he overemphasized, the extent to which 1832 had transferred power to the middle classes. Government remained primarily the business of aristocrats and gentlemen. What had changed was that the governors were now responsible to what in most, if perhaps not quite all, cases was a real electorate; but he was right that that electorate was unlikely to be sympathetic to the kinds of problems that lay behind Chartism. There was, of course, no monolithic middle-class electorate, as is sometimes suggested — indeed, as Disraeli himself sometimes suggested. Apart from anything else, in an electoral system still heavily weighted toward the agricultural South, the voices of the Chartists' enemies, the "millocrats" and the "shopocrats," were necessarily in a minority. But the fact that the bulk of the electoral power was in the hands of those to whom the problems of Chartists were largely irrelevant was not, of course, calculated to make the electorate, and hence their representatives, more responsive to those problems. So far, then, Disraeli's analysis was right; and unfortunately his own imaginative grasp of the problems of the unrepresented, and his sympathy with them, were unusual.

Yet, though there is no reason to doubt the genuineness of Disraeli's sympathy, this is not to say that it was the only, or indeed the most important, explanation of his actions. Another occasion during the same session on which he was in a minority, and a very different sort of minority, gives the clue. In March he had joined a small group of Irish Tories and extreme exponents of Protestant supremacy in opposing a government bill to reform the Irish corporations. For his own part, he disclaimed religious bigotry (though some of his earlier writings, including the *Vindication,* contain strong anti-Catholic sentiments), and based his argument solely on his concern for strong government in Ireland. He was pleased with the effect, boasting to Sarah:

> My last speech was very successful, the best *coup* I have yet made. And it was no easy task, for I spoke against the Government, the great mass of the Conservative party, and even took a different view from the small minority itself. I was listened to in silence and the utmost attention. Peel especially complimented me, sore as he was at the Conservative schism, and said, "Disraeli, you took the only proper line of opposition to the bill." . . .

The fact was that bold and unusual opinions attracted attention; and in those days of easy party discipline, occasional opposition to one's leader did no harm. Quite the contrary, daring and able men were likely to find themselves coopted into the leadership on the often sound assumption that they would be less troublesome inside than out. As his subsequent actions make quite clear, this was Disraeli's game. Some men are swept along by their sympathies — Disraeli's were always firmly controlled and regulated by his ambition.

The time, however, was not yet ripe for Disraeli, though it was for his party. In May 1841 the Whig government, long in difficulty, was finally defeated over a proposal to lower the sugar duty, which was followed by the carrying of a vote of no confidence moved by Peel. The government dissolved, but, in large part because of the fears and hostility of agriculturalists and other protected interests, they lost heavily in the general election and were forced to resign. Peel formed a Conservative government — without Disraeli.

He was bitterly disappointed. He had, he wrote to Peel, fought four contests for the party, as well as exerting "my intelligence to the utmost for the propagation of your policy. . . ." More than that, "I have had to struggle against a storm of political hate and malice which few men ever experienced, from the moment, at the instigation of a member of your Cabinet, I enrolled myself under your banner. . . ." All that had sustained him, he said, was "the conviction that the day would come when the foremost man of this country would publicly testify that he had some respect for my ability and character." He ended with an abject plea "to save me from an intolerable humiliation." Mrs. Disraeli wrote as well.

It was in vain. Peel's reply was perhaps colder and more argumentative than it needed to have been. But there is no need to doubt the sincerity of the explanation he gave, which was that, though even Peel was not tactless enough to put it so bluntly, Disraeli simply was not important enough to be included. There were too many old powers in the party who could not safely be excluded, and too many new ones, such as Disraeli's old acquaintance, Chandos, now the Duke of Buckingham but still the "Farmers' Friend," who needed to be conciliated. The claims of a relative newcomer, albeit often a bright and useful one, were simply too far down the list to be gratified. What is interesting is not Peel's decision, but Disraeli's own inflated opinion of himself and his services; for he certainly believed that he ought to have been included. As one of his opponents at Shrewsbury, whence he had removed himself for the last election, rather unkindly translated his motto — *Forti nihil difficile* — "The impudence of some men sticks at nothing."

Disraeli's opponents often charged that he deserted his leader in a fit of pique over his neglected pretensions. This is untrue, for in fact he gave Peel active support for two whole sessions. But this does not mean, as his friends have sometimes claimed, that Disraeli was swayed by the issues. The fact is that, as he was too ambitious to be led by his sympathies, so he was also too cool and shrewd to be governed by his passions. Rather, he watched and waited for his opportunity. When it came he seized it, destroying Peel in the process, though this was not necessarily his object from the beginning.

The issue which was finally to give Disraeli his chance

was the question of agricultural protection, most notably the Corn Laws. Since 1815, when Parliament attempted in effect to place an absolute prohibition on the importation of foreign grains, the question had been the source of acrimonious dispute. The price of corn (or in American usage, wheat) was necessarily of vital importance to the English consumer; for bread was still, in a very literal sense to many people, the staff of life. And the pressure of consumers, particularly the large concentrations of them in the industrial North, had led in 1828 to the adoption of a sliding scale of duties, which it was hoped would create a more flexible system. There the question rested for a while, at least as a prominent national issue. But the hard times at the end of the 1830s were bound to make it one once more. In 1838, the same year that the Chartist agitations began, the Anti–Corn Law League was founded in Manchester to promote free trade. Agitation mounted; and it was partially in response that the Whig government had proposed a lowering of duties, including a fixed 5s. duty on corn, in 1841.

As has been seen, it was in large part because of the fears of agriculturalists and other protected groups that Peel came to power. Nor can there be the least doubt that, as Disraeli later claimed, he came to power committed to the principle of protection. His own words committed him specifically, the circumstances of the election committed him morally. Nonetheless, in his very first Budget he began to whittle away at the system of protection, including a lowering of the duty on corn. His motives were the best. He hoped to promote trade by the lowering of duties, and to improve the lot of the working classes by lowering the cost of their food, thus bringing prosperity and contentment to all. Nor at this point did he intend to dismantle completely the protective system. Its exponents, however, saw the Budget as an evil portent. And, in an action that Disraeli likened to "a thunderbolt in a summer sky," the Duke of Buckingham resigned from the government. The rank and

file, promised that the 1842 reform would be final, remained loyal, but not without much grumbling and apprehension.

Disraeli gave the government his open and vocal support
on this and other matters during the session. He made what
was generally acclaimed as a particularly effective attack on
the Whig record in foreign policy in a speech on a motion
on the consular service. At the same time, however, he carefully watched the disaffection within the government ranks,
and not without calculation as to how it might serve his
own interests. On 13 March he wrote to his wife:

> I am not particularly anxious to be in town at this moment,
> political affairs are very confused; and Vyvyan [a prominent
> Protectionist], since the consular speech, always "whispering
> in my ear." Yesterday he came with a formal proposition —
> viz., to oppose the further progress of the Corn Bill to-morrow
> in consequence of Peel's financial statement. . . . I declined
> interfering, said that I hated speaking &c. &c., must watch
> events, &c. But as old Talleyrand, when he did not clearly see
> his way, always took to his bed, so I think it would be as well
> for me if, in consequence of a cause which, thank God, no
> longer exists, domestic anxiety were to take me into the coun-
> try — rather suddenly. . . .

As it turned out, Disraeli's calculations gave rise to a speech
on 10 May in which he placed Peel and his policies firmly
in the great Tory tradition of Shelburne and Pitt. But it is
evident that he could as easily have gone the other way.
The comparison with the wily old Frenchman who managed to accommodate himself to every regime, monarchical,
republican, or imperial, from Louis XVI to Louis Philippe,
was not inapt.

Disraeli took the same calculating view of the party of
young men who were now grouping themselves around him.
In the autumn he was in Paris, laying plans with two of his
new admirers, and instructing the King of the French in
current English politics. As he explained to Louis Philippe,
in the government majority of ninety there were already

between forty and fifty agricultural malcontents: "It is obvious, therefore, that another section of Conservative members full of youth and energy, and constant in their seats, must exercise an irresistible control over the tone of the Minister." He told the French King that the main use of such a party would be in foreign affairs, to influence the government in the pro-French direction he now favored; but it is safe to assume that he had other plans for it as well.

With the exception of George Smythe, who made the clearly not entirely inappropriate suggestion that the group call themselves "Diz-Union," it was genuine idealism that attracted the little band, better known as Young England, to Disraeli. They were drawn by his version of Tory radicalism, which could be, and was, made to fit with notions of their own. The two most prominent members were Smythe, son and heir of Viscount Strangford and a man of ideas, if not of ideals; and Lord John Manners, whose father was the Duke of Rutland. Smythe and Manners had been at Eton and Cambridge together; and it was at the latter place, through the missionary efforts of Frederick Faber, that they came under the influence of ideas which had their origins at the sister university. The Oxford Movement had started in the previous decade as a reaction against what many serious churchmen saw as a growing wave of secularism and Erastianism which threatened the Church's very existence. Their response to growing state interference was to stress the separate and independent existence and authority of the Church. Not surprisingly, they looked back with nostalgia to a period when such a situation had been an evident reality, as it had been in the Middle Ages. They deemphasized the Reformation as constituting no significant break in the history of the Church, and they identified with others, such as the Laudians, who had taken a similar position earlier.

The Oxford Movement, however, was a religious one, from which most of its members drew no social implications. The two Cantabrigians were exceptions. They were, of course, not unique in admiring the organic society of the Middle Ages; so did Carlyle and Ruskin, among others. But, not unnaturally, the emphasis of the young aristocrats was on the feudal monarchy and nobility, and on their central and ultimate responsibility, under the guidance of the Church, for the welfare of the rest of society. And, as they saw the Laudian Church as the last serious striving toward the medieval ideal in religious matters, so they saw the policies of Charles I and Strafford as the last attempt to enforce the ideal of the organic society, where those at the top took genuine responsibility for the welfare of those at the bottom.

These notions were now engrafted upon Disraeli's view of more recent history, with a result which he attempted to sum up in the General Preface to the 1870 collected edition of his novels. The aims of Young England were, he said:

> To change back the oligarchy into a generous aristocracy round a real throne; to infuse life and vigor into the Church, as the trainer of the nation . . . ; to establish a commercial code on the principles successfully negotiated by Lord Bolingbroke at Utrecht, and which, though baffled at the time by a Whig Parliament, were subsequently and triumphantly vindicated by his political pupil and heir, Mr. Pitt; to govern Ireland according to the policy of Charles I, and not of Oliver Cromwell; to emancipate the political constituency of 1832 from its sectarian bondage and contracted sympathies; to elevate the physical as well as the moral condition of the people, by establishing that labour required regulation as much as property; and all this rather by the use of ancient forms and the restoration of the past than by political revolutions founded on abstract ideas.

Though written almost thirty years later, and certainly in the light of what had transpired since, this is not an inaccurate summation of the ideas as they were presented in the 1840s, especially in *Coningsby* and *Sybil*, the first two volumes of the trilogy. All the notions are to be found there; but what was true of them in the years that followed was also true almost from the moment they were first enunciated, and that was that there was a wide variation in the emphasis, and more than that, in the interpretation put upon them.

Save for *Alarcos,* Disraeli's one attempt to write a play and one just as well forgotten, which had been published in 1839, he had written almost nothing since his entry into Parliament. But in the autumn of 1843, while staying with Henry Hope, a warm supporter outside Parliament, he acceded to his host's urging that he attempt to put the group's ideas into literary form. The result was *Coningsby,* published in the following year. According to Leslie Stephen, the book "wants little but a greater absence of purpose to be a first-rate novel. If Mr. Disraeli had confined himself to the merely artistic point of view, he might have drawn a picture of political society worthy of comparison with *Vanity Fair.*" Certainly, for anyone interested in the political society of the period, the novel will always have fascination. It is full of superb, if not very flattering, portraits of politicians, such as Croker and Peel, and of political caricatures, the most famous being the archetypal wirepullers Taper and Tadpole. Whether it deserves the distinction often accorded to it of being the first political novel doubtless depends on one's definition of the term. It is certainly not a political novel in the genre of Lord Snow, for it is a picture, not an analysis of behavior and motivation; and like all pictures, it is to a certain extent limited by its subject. Even Taper and Tadpole are without very recognizable analogues today. But, as a picture, drawn by an artist who knew his subject intimately, it is probably without an equal.

In this sense, the purpose, which Stephen is quite right in seeing as dominating the work, is no detriment to one's enjoyment. Harry Coningsby's grandfather, the Marquis of Monmouth, represents the bad old oligarchy of Young England's imagination, selfish and rapacious, and bending all its power to self-aggrandizement at the expense of the country's best interests. As so often is the case in Disraeli's novels, the cynical old voluptuary is, in fact, a good deal more believable and appealing than his grandson (who is a highly idealized version of that cynical young voluptuary, Smythe). The book begins with Coningsby, a young Etonian, watching the progress of the Reform Act, which his grandfather, a great aristocratic boroughmonger, naturally execrates. Coningsby does not come to love the Reform Act, but neither does he end by believing in what his grandfather sees as the new hope and bulwark of his order, the Conservative party. For, in his opinion (though the words are Taper's) "a sound Conservative government" has come to mean no more than "Tory men and Whig measures." Coningsby wants more than this. He wants "political faith . . . instead of political infidelity."

As this strong language suggests, Disraeli had moved a long way in the year that had elapsed since he had defended Peel as the heir to the free-trade policies of Shelburne and Pitt. Those policies were useful to remember in 1870 as they had been in 1842. But the notion of "commercial freedom, the germ of which may be found in the long-maligned negotiations of Utrecht, but which, in the instance of Lord Shelburne, were [sic] soon in time matured by all the economical science of Europe," is no more than adverted to by the novelist, in this case in *Sybil*. For, though Disraeli was adept at covering his change of tack, he had come to the conclusion during the course of 1843 that the prevailing winds in the party were in the Protectionist direction. He had begun the year with cautious support of the government's policy. In May, in Shrewsbury, not in Westminster, he had promised: "If I find the Government receding really from their pledges and opinions — if I find them, for instance, throwing over that landed interest that brought them into power — my vote will be recorded against them." And in the summer he duly recorded his vote against the reduction of the duty on

Canadian corn, which many saw as a sure sign that the government was throwing over the landed interest.

Yet, though Disraeli registered his vote against the government on this particular question, he did not raise his voice against it, either on the specific or general question. That would have been too quick a turn. Rather he chose to sail into opposition on a coercive measure for Ireland, which he joined his Young England colleagues in opposing. He strongly supported Smythe's contention that there were no historical grounds for the common assumption that hostility to the Irish was a characteristic of Tory policy. The policy of Charles I had been aimed at the conciliation of Irish Roman Catholicism, and that had been the thrust of Tory policy since. Wisdom and justice dictated that that should continue to be their policy. This was certainly good Young England theory. That it was good history is extremely doubtful. For, whether one looks at Charles's government in England or in Ireland, expediency is a good deal more evident than policy. So far as Tory policy was concerned, while it was true that prominent individuals, such as Pitt, Canning, and latterly Wellington and Peel, had favored conciliation, the fact was, as Catholic Emancipation had proved, that inclination could not be transformed into policy without smashing the party. Peel might have proved it again, with his policy of placing the Roman Catholic college at Maynooth on a firm financial footing; for the vote on the Maynooth Grant in 1845 marked the first massive desertion of the Prime Minister by members of his own party. Smythe and Manners supported Peel. Prominent among the leaders of the revolt was their old leader Disraeli.

This, however, is getting ahead of the story. To get back to Coningsby, were there any canons at all in the political faith he talked about? So far as the "real throne" was concerned, there was certainly a good deal of monarchical sentiment and anti-Parliamentarianism in the novel; but, while

this may have been relevant to seventeenth-century Toryism and thus dear to Young England, it had nothing whatever to do with the realities of the 1840s, and, if possible,
even less to do with the practical politics of Benjamin Disraeli. Perhaps, then, the key is in "the Church, as the trainer
of the nation"? Or, again, in the generous aristocracy, concerned with the physical as well as the moral condition of
the people, and with the regulation of labor to that end?

Predictably enough, the last set of concerns, the reestab-
lishment of a benevolent and socially responsible aristocracy, provides part of the answer. Both *Coningsby* and later
Sybil preach paternalistic concern, and not only in the
case of the nobility, as the elder Millbank, the benevolent
manufacturer who ultimately becomes Coningsby's father-
in-law, proves. Yet from Young England one would expect
that the Church would have had an important role in providing the blueprint for the ideal system of social relationships. One famous incident in *Coningsby*, the visit to the
lay abbey of St. Genevieve, built in the best revived medieval style à la Pugin, has suggested to some that this was
indeed the case. The lay abbot, Eustace Lyle, is a Catholic
convert, much admired by Lord Henry Sidney (modeled
on Lord John Manners), with whose family Coningsby is
staying. Lyle has revived the old customs, and the Sidneys
and their guest arrive to pay him a visit just as the abbey
bell sounds to summon the peasantry for the twice-weekly
almsgiving day. All is done with elaborate religious ceremony, for Lyle tells his guests "that ceremony is not, as too
commonly supposed, an idle form; I wish the people constantly and visibly to comprehend that property is their
protector and their friend." And the reader is told of the
dutiful peasantry trooping to receive largesse that "not a
heart there . . . did not bless the bell that sounded from
the tower of St. Genevieve."

The seriousness with which its creator took this touching
scene, and the notions it was calculated to evoke, is illustrated by an incident that took place several months after

it was published. He had gone down to Shrewsbury to mend political fences, and he reported to his wife that he found his constituents "a little alarmed in some quarters . . . about Popery, monasteries, and John Manners. This I shall quietly soften down. . . ." Medievalism, and the social theories derived from it, were not a serious part of Disraeli's intellectual cargo, but merely ballast to be taken on or discarded as necessary.

Sybil, published exactly a year after *Coningsby* in May 1845, does not indulge much in theoretical constructs. It is true that the opening scene takes place in the ruins of an old abbey, and that Sybil and her father, the true spokesman of popular sentiments, were of the "old faith." But this was not central to the main purpose of the work. As Disraeli himself said in 1870, "in SYBIL, OR THE TWO NATIONS, I considered the condition of the people, and the whole work, generally speaking, was devoted to that portion of my scheme. . . ." The novel was a triumph of sympathetic understanding, based partly on personal observation during a trip to Manchester in the summer of 1844, but probably more on an exhaustive study of the bluebooks containing the official reports of various investigations into the condition of the laboring classes, and of the correspondence of the Chartist leader Feargus O'Connor obtained for Disraeli by his friend the Radical M.P. Thomas Duncombe. *Sybil*, like *Coningsby* before it, was an immediate and immense success. And it was a major contribution to the important task of identifying, and directing public attention toward, the growing fissure in English society between the Two Nations, "THE RICH AND THE POOR." It proposed no solutions, however. The hero, Charles Egremont, whose speech on the Chartist petition is more than reminiscent of Disraeli's own, is a sympathetic aristocrat; but there is little hint as to what practical direction his sympathy might take.

It is only fair to Disraeli and Young England to say that as active politicians their sympathy took very practical

forms. Disraeli's opposition to the New Poor Law continued. In 1841, when the Whig government moved its renewal
for another ten years, Disraeli moved for rejection. The bill
was lost through the dissolution; and, though Disraeli did
not vocally oppose the efforts of his own leaders at renewal
the following year, he remained aloof from those efforts,
and on one occasion voted against the government. In 1847
he was to speak and vote against renewal. Similarly,
throughout the 1840s, and in 1844 against official government policy, Disraeli supported the efforts of the future
Lord Shaftesbury to limit the hours and regulate the conditions of factory workers.

Yet, though what Disraeli some years later described as
"the Young England myth" would exercise a powerful influence on the future of the Conservative party, neither the
myth nor the reality of Young England was Disraeli's major
preoccupation during the 1840s. In the summer of 1844 he
talked to his constituents at Shrewsbury about his motives
for entering public life; he was prepared to "candidly ac-
knowledge" that "I love fame; I love public reputation; I
love to live in the eyes of the country; and it is a glorious
thing for a man to do who has had my difficulties to con-
tend against." His ambition was about to receive new gratification. He was about to become, as he said in a continua-
tion of the remarks about Young England quoted above,
"if not the recognised leader, at least the most influential
organ, of a powerful parliamentary party."

That party was not Young England, which had never
had more than three or four regular adherents and perhaps
as many more occasional ones; and the position Disraeli
achieved in it had nothing to do with Young England's
ideals, though it did arise from the breaking of that Conservative party against which Young England had so elo-
quently inveighed. But his chance did not come from the
young and eloquent, but from the old and inarticulate
Protectionist wing of the party — they desperately needed
an organ.

The leadership of Young England, and the notoriety far out of proportion to its small numbers that this gained him, had helped to mark him out for the place. He had also gained greatly in parliamentary manners and judgment. In speaking he had adopted a style which rigorously eschewed the dramatic. He began impassive, almost monotonous. As he approached a point, he became more animated, but he still studiously underplayed his role. As *Fraser's Magazine* described him in 1847:

> While all around him are convulsed with merriment or excitement at some of his finely-wrought sarcasms, he holds himself, seemingly, in total suspension, as though he had no existence for the ordinary feelings and passions of humanity; and the moment the shouts and confusion have subsided, the same calm, low, monotonous, but yet distinct and searching voice, is heard still pouring forth his ideas, while he is preparing to launch another sarcasm, hissing hot, into the soul of his victim.

It was in this fashion that he hunted Peel and destroyed him. The speech on the Irish measure at the end of the 1843 session was followed by another attack, this time on the government's Eastern policy, a few days later. Peel was furious, and was absolutely incredulous at the end of the year when Disraeli asked for an office for one of his brothers. The request was refused, and Disraeli was not sent the usual circular requesting the attendance of government supporters at the beginning of the 1844 session. When one remembers that he was in the middle of writing *Coningsby,* it seems most unlikely to say the least that Disraeli was contemplating loyal support. Nonetheless, he protested the omission and actually spoke for a government measure on Ireland early in the session.

Peel, of course, could not have known about Disraeli's literary pursuits, and can perhaps be accused of overreacting. But he was particularly vulnerable to Disraeli's attacks, and the latter was particularly adept at searching out the chinks in his armor, as this session and the next two were to demonstrate conclusively. As discontent mounted in his own party, Peel, confident of his own motives and scornful of those who would not share them, became increasingly withdrawn from and imperious with his followers. On two occasions during the 1844 session, once over the Factory Bill, and a second time over a preference which had been voted to free-grown colonial sugar over slave-grown foreign sugar, he demanded that the House reverse itself. Disraeli seized the occasion for a particularly strong and defiant speech, and a memorable sarcasm. The Prime Minister, he said, professed a horror of slavery, but it seemed to stop short of the benches behind him. "There the gang is still assembled, and there the thong of the whip still sounds." He sat down amidst tremendous applause from both sides of the House, while his own front bench sat in pained silence; and one observer, the future Lord Broughton, claimed that he had never seen Peel and his colleagues "look so wretched."

They were to look more wretched still in the next session, for then Disraeli hammered a theme on which Peel was almost morbidly sensitive — apostasy. Sometimes Peel himself assisted, as on one occasion when he quoted Canning against Disraeli: "Save, save, O save me, from the candid friend!" In a crushing retort, Disraeli reminded the House that this was the man, the hope of the High Protestants, who had deserted Canning on the issue of Catholic Emancipation, only to reverse himself and play a leading part in carrying the question not long afterwards. If anyone had failed to draw the connection, Disraeli made it explicit a fortnight later on a motion to relieve agricultural distress. Significantly enough, he was responding to some remarks made a few days earlier by Sidney Herbert, which, though he could not have known it, had been occasioned by Peel's conversion to free trade. Richard Cobden, the great champion of free trade, had taxed Peel with not accepting the full logic of his position. Peel turned to Herbert, who was sitting next to him, and said: "You must answer this, for I

cannot." Herbert did so, and in the process made the unfortunate comment that it was "distasteful to the agriculturalists to come whining to Parliament at every period of
temporary distress." Disraeli did not let the remark pass:

> The right hon. gentleman [Peel], being compelled to inter-
> fere, sends down his valet, who says in the genteelest manner:
> "We can have no whining here." And that, sir, is exactly the
> case of the great agricultural interest — that beauty which
> everybody wooed and one deluded. There is a fatality in such
> charms, and we now seem to approach the catastrophe of her
> career. Protection appears to be in about the same condition
> that Protestantism was in 1828. The country will draw its
> moral.

And he concluded by expressing "thus publicly my belief
that a Conservative Government is an organised hypocrisy."

This was in March 1845. Events moved fast in the latter
part of the year. The famous Irish potato famine necessi-
tated the opening of the ports to foreign corn to supple-
ment the food supply of the British Isles. Peel was convinced
that, once opened, they could never be closed again; that
is, that the repeal of the Corn Laws was the only alternative
to massive internal discontent and disorder. In December
he resigned; but the Whigs were not eager to grasp the
nettle, and Peel, who was perhaps too eager, came back
again.

Save for Lord Stanley, Peel's colleagues came back with
him. He remained the head of a strong and talented ministry, and in the opening debate on 22 January 1846 he
acted the part, calm, confident, and full of detail. He
seemed so fully in control that he almost remained so, for
the country members were disorganized and dumb, helpless
in the face of his talent and expertise. It was in such a situation, with the crafty prey almost out of danger, that Disraeli
rose to deliver his great lacerating sarcasm:

> Sir, there is a difficulty in finding a parallel to the position
> of the right hon. gentleman in any part of history. The only

parallel which I can find is an incident in the late war in the Levant. . . . I remember when that great struggle was taking place, when the existence of the Turkish Empire was at stake, the Sultan, a man of great energy and fertile in resources, was determined to fit out an immense fleet to maintain his empire. Accordingly a vast armament was collected. The crews were picked men, the officers were the ablest men that could be found. . . . There never was an armament which left the Dardanelles similarly appointed since the days of Solyman the Great. The Sultan personally witnessed the departure of the fleet; and the muftis prayed for the expedition, as all the muftis here prayed for the success of the last general election. Away went the fleet, but what was the Sultan's consternation when the Lord High Admiral steered at once into the enemy's port. (Loud laughter and cheers.) Now, sir, the Lord High Admiral on that occasion was very much misrepresented. He, too, was called a traitor, and he, too, vindicated himself. "True it is," said he, "I did place myself at the head of this valiant armada; true it is that my Sovereign embraced me; true it is that all the muftis in the empire offered up prayers for the expedition; but I have an objection to war. I see no use in prolonging the struggle, and the only reason I had for accepting the command was that I might terminate the contest by betraying my master." (Tremendous Tory cheering.)

Disraeli had drawn blood. The "gentlemen of England" were in full cry, baying at his back. They would not halt until they had run their quarry to the ground and destroyed him.

FOUR

Leadership Consolidated

As HAS BEEN SEEN, Disraeli described his position about this time as "if not the recognised leader, at least the most influential organ, of a powerful parliamentary party." It is an accurate and highly significant distinction. For though Disraeli served as the most powerful and effective spokesman of the two-thirds or so of the Conservative party who could not follow Peel in his new course, and thus fulfilled one of the most important functions of a leader, he was not yet recognized as such. It was to be several years before the "gentlemen of England" came even close to accepting this exotic adventurer, with his erratic and somewhat dubious past, as their chief in the House of Commons.

The leadership of the Protectionist party as a whole was conceded to the only important leader of the old party who had not followed Peel, Lord Stanley, an ex-Whig but strong supporter of the Church and the landed interest, who had gravitated to Conservatism in the thirties. The lead in the Commons went to the scion of another great landed family, Lord George Bentinck, a son of the Duke of Portland. Like Stanley, Bentinck also came from a Canningite-Whiggish background (the two strains had tended to blend in the late twenties and early thirties), but he too was a strong exponent of the landed interest and had been shocked and disgusted by Peel's desertion of that interest. Indeed that desertion so revolted him that he left his real loves, the hunting field and the turf, to take up the burdens of leading a party. "I keep horses in three counties," he said, "and they tell me that I shall save fifteen hundred a year by free trade. I don't care for that: what I cannot bear is being sold."

Bentinck was to be a not ineffective leader, in part because of the obvious strength of his feelings. But it was not Bentinck who had first given voice to the passion that was now the great moving force within him. As he later confessed, when in the session of 1845 Disraeli "predicted and denounced the impending defection of the Minister, there was no member of the Conservative party who more violently condemned the unfounded attack, or more readily impugned the motives of the assailant." Disraeli had been the prophet of Peel's apostasy, and it was his eloquence that had firmly fixed the brand upon him. There can be no doubt that the passion would have existed without him; but there must be real doubt that it would have reached the same heights of bitterness, or even have been very effective without the leadership he gave.

To a greater extent than historians are now generally willing to admit, the bitterness against Peel was justified. It is true that Peel acted from the highest and most disinterested motives, that Parliament was not yet representative of the nation as a whole, and that a majority of the general public would probably have endorsed Peel's action. There were very few, however (including Peel himself), who would have endorsed the assumption from which Peel seemed to proceed, that it was the duty of the government to decide the best interests of the country, and the duty of their party to follow wherever they might lead. Most people believed that parties stood for broad principles and policies; and no one would have doubted that the Con-

servatives were preeminently the party of the Church and
the landed interest. It was, of course, possible to disagree
about how the interests of Church and Land could best be
served. But, as the votes on both the Maynooth Grant and
the Corn Laws proved, a large majority of Peel's own party
believed that he was acting against those interests. Such being the case, Peel's actions must be held in part responsible
for a growing belief in the faithlessness of politicians, which
was to be one cause of the political instability in the decade
and a half that followed. Bentinck was not alone in his
feeling of revulsion against the way Peel had acted. To
many people his argument that the Whigs' refusal of office
left him no choice lacked conviction; and they believed,
probably rightly, that Russell, who had already endorsed
free trade in corn, could have been made to take office had
Peel not been so anxious to relieve him of his difficulties in
forming a government. Distrust of the rectitude of politicians is not healthy in any polity, and, to the extent that
Peel was responsible for such feelings in his own time, he
must bear the blame.

To apportion blame is not easy, but it is certain that the
man who had taken it upon himself to censor Peel added
immensely to the distrust and confusion which doubtless
had their origin in the latter's action. It was Disraeli himself who later recorded the following version of an exchange
between the Queen and Stanley in 1851, when there was a
real possibility that a Protectionist government would be
formed:

> The Queen said: "I always felt that, if there were a Protec-
> tionist Government, Mr. D. must be the Leader of the House
> of Commons: but I do not approve of Mr. D. I do not ap-
> prove of his conduct to Sir Robert Peel."
> Lord Derby [Stanley] said: "Madam, Mr. D. has had to
> make his position, and men who make their positions will say
> and do things which are not necessary to be said or done by
> those for whom positions are provided."
> "That is true," said the Queen. "And all I can now hope is

that, having attained this great position, he will be temper-
ate."

More than one politician has been excused on the grounds
that he had to make his own way to the top; and of more
than one has the pious hope been expressed that, having
fought his way to the top, he will somehow become different, a statesman rather than merely a scheming politician.
Very often the excuse is unjustified and the hope disappointed. So far as Disraeli is concerned, the fulfillment of
the hope, or lack of it, will be considered in due course. We
shall now turn our attention to what he said and did in his
final climb to the top. Just what kind of leader did the
gentlemen of England finally get? What principles, if any,
guided his actions?

For the balance of the 1846 session those principles
seemed to be pretty much the ones he had espoused for the
past two years. What is usually known as the repeal of the
Corn Laws, though it was actually a progressive lowering
of the duty to a purely nominal one over the course of
three years, was carried, despite the best efforts of Disraeli
and the other Protectionist leaders, by Peel with Whig-
Radical support. But on 25 June, on the same night that
the Corn question was safely carried in the Lords, Peel was
defeated on an Irish Coercion Bill by a combination of Protectionist, Whig, Radical, and Irish votes. Probably only
the Corn question had saved him from an earlier defeat,
when Whigs joined the Protectionists in almost carrying a
Ten Hours Bill; that is, a bill to limit the hours of factory
workers to ten a day. Peel resigned, to be replaced by Russell and a minority Whig government existing on Peelite
sufferance. As for Disraeli, he had continued to act on the
combination of Protectionist, Tory radical, and Irish conciliation principles that he had recently espoused — albeit
not always acted on, as, for example, in the case of the Maynooth Grant.

Disraeli was later to argue, and his admirers have contended since, that there was nothing in his speeches in the parliamentary sessions of 1845 and 1846 that actually committed him to protection, and that what he was criticizing was not Peel's economics but his desertion of his principles. While the speeches were undoubtedly mainly an invective on Peel's apostasy, the distinction is a fine one (and, it might be added, one lost on his contemporaries). There can be no doubt whatever, however, about the meaning of remarks he made at a series of Protectionist meetings around the country during the summer. At these meetings he explicitly held out the promise of regaining efficient protection, and even of repealing the act just passed. The latter prospect was held out at King's Lynn, where, as he had written to his wife, "if we are to be reported in *The Times* it must be something for the nation, and not merely for the farmers of Lynn." It is evident that he was not merely carried away by the enthusiasm of the yokels. He meant to create the impression that the leading Protectionist spokesman actually believed in protection.

Protection was not, however, to dominate the next session, as all the leaders of the party agreed that it was too soon to act for a reversal of the previous year's measure. It was Ireland, still suffering from the effects of the devastating famine, that monopolized attention. Disraeli, sensibly enough, advocated economic intervention, in the form of railway building and other productive public works, to help meet the problem; and, though he was never to act on his own principles when given the opportunity, the Whig government ultimately made some moves in this direction. Disraeli also continued his criticism of the Poor Law and his advocacy of local control of relief. And he gave steady and efficient support to Bentinck on a number of other questions.

Observers noted that Disraeli began in every way to appear more sober and responsible. At the beginning of the session, the Protectionists, whose remaining on the government side had forced many of the ministry's own followers to sit opposite, followed the Peelites across the floor. The leaders took their seats on the same front bench as Peel, with Disraeli only three away from the man whom he, more than anyone else, had hounded from office. Disraeli took on an appearance and demeanor appropriate to his new seat. According to a provincial journalist, the "motley-coloured garments" were replaced by a black suit "unapproachably perfect" in every detail, "and he appears to have doffed the vanity of the coxcomb with the plumage of the peacock."

The general election of 1847 added more weight and dignity to his position, for he now secured the envied distinction of becoming member for a county, his own beloved Buckinghamshire. He was generally believed to be the candidate, and his enemies charged him with being the nominee, of his old friend the Duke of Buckingham. The Duke was teetering on the brink of the abyss of financial disaster, into which he was soon to fall; but the name of the "Farmers' Friend" was still one to conjure with, and his minions could still, and did, give powerful support. There would have been every reason for them to do so, for Disraeli was a candidate very much in the Duke's tradition, as an election card put it in describing him and two other candidates, an opponent of "Popery" and a friend to agriculture. In accordance with the policy adopted the previous session, one apparently acceptable to the electorate, protection was not emphasized. But there was strong anti-Catholic feeling among the electors, and Disraeli took full advantage of it, stressing his opposition to the endowment of the Catholic clergy and his vote against the Maynooth Grant.

The banners under which Disraeli rode to success at Aylesbury in August were highly appropriate for a leader of the Protectionist party, which was drawn from traditionally High Protestant elements and had earlier been led by men, such as the Dukes of Buckingham and Richmond, who were devoted to both causes. But the standard under which the new member for Buckinghamshire was to appear at Westminster soon after Parliament assembled in the autumn was most inappropriate and highly embarrassing. The cause of the difficulty was Disraeli's intimate friend and Buckinghamshire neighbor, generally known by his Austrian title of "Baron" Lionel de Rothschild. In the election Rothschild, a practicing Jew, had been returned by the City of London; and it was generally expected that his colleague for the City, the Prime Minister, an old supporter of Jewish relief, would press the issue. The result was bound to be distressing, not only to Disraeli, but also to Bentinck, who, while he had left the Whigs, had brought his Whiggish views on civil and religious liberty with him.

Perhaps not unnaturally, Disraeli hoped the whole thing would go away. As he wrote to the still loyal Manners (Smythe had followed Peel) on 16 November:

> The peril is not so imminent. It is even on the cards that the Bill will be introduced in the Lords; and whatever the result there, it will be a great relief to us. But if introduced into the Commons, Lord John will only give notice before Christmas, and the battle is not to be fought until next year. Lionel, as at present counselled, will not even take his seat to choose the Speaker.

Disraeli was to be disappointed. For on 16 December Russell moved that the House should go into Committee "on the removal of the civil and political disabilities affecting Her Majesty's Jewish subjects." The battle was joined, and Disraeli was in the forefront. On the first day of the debate he rose and delivered a powerful speech in favor of the motion. His grounds, however, were entirely his own. The other advocates of the measure, including his own leader, Bentinck, advanced the old arguments of civil and religious liberty, agreeing with Russell in his contention "that every Englishman born in the country is entitled to all the honours and advantages of the British Constitution," and that religious opinions should be no bar. Disraeli took a very different line. He argued not that the Jews should not be punished for their opinions, but quite the contrary that they should be honored and embraced precisely because of those opinions:

> The very reason for admitting the Jews is because they can show so near an affinity to you. Where is your Christianity if you do not believe in their Judaism? Do not mix up, then, the consideration of a question which is so intimately allied to your own faith, with the different considerations that would apply to the Pagan and the Mahommedan. I am prepared to lay down the broadest principles as to the importance of maintaining a Christian character in this House and in this country; and yet it is on this very ground you will found and find the best argument for the admission of the Jews.

Arguments such as these give the lie to interpretations of Disraeli, such as Cecil Roth's, which see him as having a natural sympathy with the oppressed because of his own origins in an oppressed race. His sympathies were distinctly limited, and he was not in the least concerned with the plight of other oppressed minorities. Indeed, in 1854 he was to oppose a very similar measure because, besides providing for the relief of Jews, it also altered the oaths in a way which he thought favored Roman Catholics and those who sympathized with them within the Anglican church. Nor, as has been seen and will be seen further, did Disraeli ever hesitate to exploit religious bigotry, whether against Catholics, Anglo-Catholics, or Protestant Dissenters, whenever he thought it would be to his political advantage.

It is important, then, not to misunderstand the grounds on which Disraeli argued for the Jews. He did not object to the principle of exclusion, as such; he simply thought the Jews had a special claim to be included:

> Is it not the first business of the Christian Church to make the population whose mind she attempts to form, and whose morals she seeks to guide, acquainted with the history of the Jews? . . . On every sacred day you read to the people the exploits of Jewish heroes, the proofs of Jewish devotion, the brilliant annals of past Jewish magnificence. The Christian

Church has covered every kingdom with sacred buildings, and over every altar . . . we find the tables of the Jewish law. Every Sunday — every Lord's day — if you wish to express feelings of praise and thanksgiving to the Most High, or if you wish to find expression of solace in grief, you find both in the words of the Jewish poets. . . . All the early Christians were Jews. The Christian religion was first preached by men who had been Jews until they were converted; every man in the early ages of the Church by whose power, or zeal, or genius, the Christian faith was propagated, was a Jew.

All this, of course, was perfectly true. But, among his colleagues in the House, whose Christian tradition had stressed other Jews who persecuted and impeded, it was extremely unpopular. Disraeli, however, was only stirred to greater heights of defiant eloquence by the obvious and vocal signs of disapproval that accompanied his remarks:

> I cannot sit in this House with any misconception of my opinion on the subject. Whatever may be the consequences on the seat I hold . . . I cannot, for one, give a vote which is not in deference to what I believe to be the true principles of religion. Yes, it is as a Christian that I will not take upon me the awful responsibility of excluding from the legislature those who are of the religion in the bosom of which my Lord and Saviour was born.

Disraeli's biographers have accepted his stand on Jewish relief as he portrayed it — one of disinterested courage. That it was courageous can hardly be doubted, but whether it was disinterested is another matter. What was the alternative? It is usually argued that policy would have dictated that he should have abstained or absented himself from the debate, thus avoiding angering the squires on the back benches and endangering his precarious new position as one of the leaders of a great party. Such a strategy might have worked for Bentinck, and it is greatly to his credit that he did not pursue it. But would it have worked for a man whose Jewish birth was well known, and, as we shall see, only just blatantly advertised once again in *Tancred?* It seems more likely that, while gaining him little or nothing with the squires, such a course would have laid him open to such devastating sneers from his enemies as in the end to have weakened his credit with all parties. Though politicians are often slow to grasp the fact, there are times when courage and policy are the same thing. Disraeli, as Gladstone was to testify after his death, was rarely lacking in courage, or, as Gladstone probably meant to imply, in calculation. This would seem to have been one of those occasions when the two qualities were combined.

As has been seen, Disraeli had been confronted with the anomaly of Jewish birth combined with Tory politics almost from the moment he took his seat in Parliament in 1837. On that occasion, he had sidestepped the issue. But what was possible for an obscure backbencher was impossible for a party leader; and in any case this was not Disraeli's way. When confronted with a difficult fact, he might meet it with a bold-faced lie, as he had done in categorically denying that he had ever solicited office from Peel when the latter taxed him on the matter during one of the final great debates of the spring of 1846. But evasion was not his style, certainly not on the question of his origins. As he contemptuously remarked of his grandmother, in a memoir of his father written a year or two after the debates, she "had imbibed that dislike for her race which the vain are too apt to adopt when they find that they are born to public contempt." He would not make the same mistake of trying to deny his birth.

Rather Disraeli tried to make his birth fit his new position. He constructed a fantastic pedigree tracing his descent from the aristocratic Jewish families of Spain; and it was the appearance of his new crest, the Castle of Castile, at Shrewsbury in 1841 that provided the occasion for the remarks on his motto and its impudence. In the memoir of Isaac quoted above, which was published in 1849 as a preface to his father's collected works, Disraeli fleshed out the pedigree. The Spanish Jews, he tells us, appeared by a decree of Constantine as "owners and cultivators of the soil, a circumstance which alone proves the antiquity and nobility of their settlement, for the possession of land is never conceded to a degraded race." They prospered in Spain, under the Moors after the Romans, and by the time the Inquisition was introduced to Spain at the end of the fourteenth century two-thirds of the nobility of Aragon were Jews. But the new religious zeal hounded them out, and they fled, becoming "the main source of Italian Jews, and of the most respectable portion of the Jews of Holland." Those who fled to Italy, the account goes on, settled mainly in Venice; and among them, of course, were his own ancestors, who "grateful to the God of Jacob who had sustained them through unheard-of perils . . . assumed the name of Disraeli, a name never borne before or since by any other family, in order that their race might be for ever recognised."

This elaborate pedigree was without any basis in fact: Disraeli's family were from Cento, near Ferrara, where they engaged in the straw bonnet trade, and were entirely innocent of any Spanish forebears. But, fictional though it was, at least so far as Disraeli was concerned, this imagined ancestry served as the basis of one of his favorite theories. Already in *Coningsby*, Sidonia, the all-wise financier who is a blend of Rothschild and Disraeli himself, had informed his eager young pupil that the Jews "are essentially Tories." In *Tancred*, which completed the trilogy, the theory is taken a good deal further. Here we are told that "the native tendency of the Jewish race, who are justly proud of their blood, is against the doctrine of the equality of man. They have also another characteristic, the faculty of acquisition. . . . Thus it will be seen that all the tendencies of the Jewish race are conservative. Their bias is to religion, property, and natural aristocracy. . . ." Disraeli, then, portrayed himself as coming from the most aristocratic branch of an aristocratic race, more tory than the Tories. And Disraeli's race had been great and powerful, while the Anglo-

Saxon race was in the process of being "spawned, perhaps, in the morasses of some Northern forest hardly yet cleared." That put the English aristocracy in the proper perspective.

Yet, striking though these notions on the connection of aristocracy and Jewishness are, they have to vie with other at least equally original and startling ideas. For it is in *Tancred*, published in March 1847, that Disraeli took furthest the themes that he would pursue in the December debates. Tancred, Lord Montacute, is the only child of the Duke of Bellamont. His father intends the young man for the normal apprenticeship of a future peer in the Commons. But Tancred is not content to follow conventional paths. Recalling a crusading Montacute, he says: "It is time to restore and renovate our communications with the Most High. I, too, would kneel at that tomb; I, too, surrounded by the holy hills and sacred groves of Jerusalem, would relieve my spirit from the bale that bows it down; would lift up my voice to heaven, and ask, What is DUTY, and what is FAITH? What ought I to DO, and what ought I to BELIEVE?" Not entirely surprisingly, his fond parents can make little of all this, and perhaps more surprisingly, neither can a bishop who is called in for his counsel. But Sidonia understands perfectly: "It appears to me, Lord Montacute, that what you want is to penetrate the great Asian mystery."

Precisely what the "great Asian mystery" was has, to a certain extent, always remained one. Disraeli later said that *Tancred* completed the purpose of the trilogy by treating the role of the Church, which Young England saw as "a main remedial agency in our present state." But, as Disraeli himself said, Young England was by this time a "myth" already evaporated, and we hear nothing about the "old faith," and precious little about the modern Church for that matter. Nor, aside from the crusading ancestor, is there anything about the Middle Ages. Rather, Disraeli concentrates on developing his theme of the Jewish prototype — this roughly is the "great Asian mystery" — of all that he sees as best in modern society. More particularly, he dwells on the Jewish contribution to Christianity. The general line of the argument is the same as that advanced in the December debates, but with some extraordinary embellishments. The most memorable is the question put in the mouth of the Jewish heroine, Eva: "Now tell me: suppose the Jews had not prevailed upon the Romans to crucify Jesus, what would have become of the Atonement?" A good question, but one that it would have been more tactful not to ask.

Unfortunately, one cannot leave *Tancred* without at least alluding to Disraeli's views on race. Once again, Sidonia is the protagonist:

> Is it what you call civilization that makes England flourish? Is it the universal development of the faculties of man that has rendered an island, almost unknown to the ancients, the arbiter of the world? Clearly not. It is her inhabitants that have done this; it is an affair of race. A Saxon race, protected by an insular position, has stamped its diligent and methodic character on the century. . . . *All is race;* there is no other truth.

The idea had the usual distasteful concomitants: "What would be the consequence on the great Anglo-Saxon republic . . . were its citizens to secede from their sound principle of reserve, and mingle with their negro and coloured populations?"

The Jews were an elder branch of the superior Caucasian peoples. They too maintained the purity of their blood, and so forth. His notions of race were to remain with Disraeli to the end of his days, and are reflected in his last novel, *Endymion.* But in fairness to Disraeli it must be pointed out that such ideas were far from unique. Nor, probably, did his espousal of them have much effect on anyone, including himself. *Tancred* was not a great popular success. As for its author, it is difficult to see his doctrine of race, as such, exercising much influence on his career. His admiration of the achievements of the Jewish people, and the perception of himself — or more accurately, myth — that he built around it are undoubtedly central to his life.

The racist notions that floated around that admiration were not. If Disraeli subscribed to any theory of greatness it was to the heroic principle of Carlyle, with its emphasis on the supremely talented individual who can surmount all obstacles and dominate the world, a man like Napoleon — and, he hoped, himself.

Dreams of grandeur, however, cannot have been uppermost in Disraeli's mind at this juncture in his career. His immediate problem was to secure his highly precarious position in his own party. The stand of their leaders on the Jewish question was intensely unpopular with the rank and file. When the Chief Whip intimated the discontent to Bentinck, who had risen from his sickbed to support his convictions and his lieutenant, Lord George, rejoicing "like a caged wild bird escaped from his wired prison," immediately resigned. Who was to take his place? "Nobody can think of a successor to Bentinck," wrote Greville in January 1848, "and, bad as he is, he seems the best man they have. It seems they detest Disraeli, the only man of talent, and in fact they have nobody."

They had, however, to have somebody. And Disraeli had the great advantage that had put him forward in the first place — they had nobody else. The rest were too old or too young, too ill, too uninterested, or, in the vast majority of cases, simply too incompetent. But the party would not yet officially recognize the facts. In February Lord John Manners's elder brother, the Marquis of Granby, was chosen leader without opposition. He resigned almost immediately, and for the rest of the session the party was in theory leaderless, but with Disraeli acting as its most eloquent and effective spokesman. His task was greatly aided by a variety of problems, a monetary crisis, the continuing effects of famine in Ireland, the disastrous results of free trade policies on an already declining West Indian economy, and a trade depression. The details need not detain us; but the general solution which Disraeli advanced for the economic ills of the country was moderate protection and reciprocity.

Disraeli's effectiveness was generally acknowledged, and at Stanley's request he summed up for the party at the end of the session. Still, however, the party was not ready for him. In September Bentinck dropped dead, appropriately enough on a country walk; and Lord Malmesbury, the future Foreign Secretary, confided to his diary: "No one but Disraeli can fill his place. . . . It will leave [him] without a rival, and enable him to show the great genius he undoubtedly possesses without any comparisons." Stanley, while recognizing Disraeli's genius, was not so sure. The Chief Whip confirmed his reservations; he had, he said, been warned repeatedly not to trust Disraeli, and while he could point to nothing in his conduct to justify such suspicion, "I can scarcely help believing there must be some foundation for so general an opinion as I have alluded to. . . ."

Stanley would have preferred Granby, but the latter was still reluctant. He then hit upon John Charles Herries, an elderly financier, who had served Canning and sat in Goderich's ill-fated Cabinet twenty-odd years before. At the end of December he tried out the idea on Disraeli. "I am doing you bare justice," Stanley wrote, "when I say that as a debater there is no one of our party who can pretend to compete with you; and the powers of your mind, your large general information, and the ability you possess to make yourself both heard and felt, must at all times give you a commanding position in the House of Commons, and a preponderating influence in the party to which you are attached." But, believing that "your formal establishment in the post of Leader would not meet with a general and cheerful approval on the part of those with whom you are acting," he proposed that Disraeli defer to Herries's leadership.

There could be no mistaking the reply:

I am not insensible, especially in this age, to the principle of duty — but in the present distracted state of parties, it is my

opinion, however erroneous, that I could do more to uphold
the cause to which I am attached, that I should have better
opportunities of reviving the spirit, and raising the general
tone of feeling throughout the country, by acting alone and
unshackled, than if I fell into the party discipline, which you
intimate.

Stanley knew full well that such "independent support,"
especially from Disraeli, could be worse than outright opposition, and, as Disraeli persisted in his attitude, he had no
choice but to give in. The solution was a triumvirate, the
leadership being vested in a committee composed of Herries, Granby, and Disraeli. "Sieyes, Roger Ducos, and Napoleon Bonaparte," commented Lord Aberdeen. He was
right. As Napoleon soon soared above his two colleagues, so
did Disraeli above his. He now had official recognition,
and, whatever the theoretical niceties, from January 1849
he was the effective leader of the Protectionist party in the
House of Commons.

In the same letter to Stanley just referred to, Disraeli
said that "the office of leader of the Conservative party in
the H. of C., at the present day, is to uphold the aristocratic
settlement of this country. That is the only question at
stake. . . ." Lord Blake has made much of this statement,
remarking that "this assertion is the key to Disraeli's policy
for the rest of his life. It represented his profoundest conviction and, through all the labyrinthine twists and turns
of his bewildering policy, it remained to the end his guid-
ing purpose." Blake says he meant not those who might
immediately come to mind when the word aristocracy is
mentioned, the great noble families, for they tended to be
Whiggish and cosmopolitan, but rather the kind of ordered hierarchy which prevailed in his own county of Buckinghamshire. Some local grandee, as Lord Lieutenant,
usually occupied the pinnacle of the social pyramid; but
the solid upper reaches, of which the pinnacle was only an
ornament, were comprised of the squirearchy of varying
degree, men who as J.P.'s administered justice, had once

administered the Poor Law, and were generally responsible for the governance of the county and the welfare of its inhabitants. He had in mind, then, according to Blake, those solid landowning families who stood behind what he elsewhere called the "territorial constitution," and who both in their private and their public capacities made it work, the country gentlemen — or, in Disraeli's own words, "the gentlemen of England."

That Disraeli did not have in mind the nobility may perhaps be believed. As he has the elder Millbank say in *Coningsby:* "We owe the English peerage to three sources: the spoilation of the church; the open and flagrant sale of its honours by the elder Stuarts; and the boroughmongering of our own times." Millbank goes on to say, "They have neither the right of the Normans, nor do they fulfil the duty of the Normans: they did not conquer the land, and they do not defend it." Disraeli equates the nobility with the rapacious oligarchy, irresponsible and self-interested. Nor does he, as Blake seems to suggest, at any rate in his fictional and theoretical works, make any distinction between parties. The Marquis of Monmouth and his friends were, after all, Conservatives, and saw that party as the new hope of their order. "The New Generation" (*Coningsby*'s subtitle) was to regenerate, not just the Whigs, but the aristocracy as a whole.

But whether Disraeli actually had such a devotion as Blake suggests to the squirearchy and their interests, much less made them the lodestar of his future career, is highly doubtful. Like most historians of the period, Blake makes the mistake of seeing the squirearchy as a separate and independent class, dominating the countryside and swaying it according to its own interests. Disraeli never made such a mistake. As he had told his constituents at Shrewsbury in 1843:

Gentlemen, when I talk of the preponderance of the landed interest, do not for a moment suppose that I mean merely the

> preponderance of "squires of high degree." My thought wan-
> ders farther than a lordly tower or a baronial hall. I am look-
> ing in that phrase . . . to the population of our innumerable
> villages, to the crowds in our rural towns. . . . I [also] mean
> the great estate of the Church. . . .

And toward the very end of his life, he would boast to
Lady Bradford that, by preventing the Lords from throwing
out a modification of the Game Laws which was very popular with the farmers, he had prevented the alienation of a
critical section of "the only classes on wh. we once thought
we cd. rely — the landed interest in all its divisions."

When all is said and done, it will most likely be found
that what distinguished the squires on the Conservative, or
Protectionist, back benches from their opponents was primarily the sort of constituency for which they sat. For the
Conservatives had no monopoly on country squires, any
more than the Whigs had on the nobility. It was simply
that the Conservatives tended to sit for places, generally
counties and smaller towns, where "the landed interest in
all its divisions" predominated. The Conservative party
was not the party of the squires; it was the party of the
countryside and the smaller towns, which not unnaturally
chose leading residents and neighbors, the squires, as representatives.

In the sense that, largely through his own efforts in
ousting the Peelites, the party Disraeli came to lead in 1849
was made up predominantly of squires (and peers) repre-
senting the landed interest, and that, despite his best efforts,
the party continued to have such a composition and bias
throughout the period in which he led it, it is doubtless
correct to see much of his policy as aimed at preserving the
"aristocratic settlement" in its broadest sense. Any other
course would have been political suicide. But to see such
a course as based on any more than this kind of ultimate
opportunism is, as will be seen, extremely difficult.

Certainly he had a very low opinion of the "gentlemen of
England" as represented in the House of Commons. As he

wrote to Manners of a debate shortly after he became their leader, he had attempted to keep down the "old trash." But of the new men he tried to bring forward, "I could scarcely get one of them out." He went on: "Alas! alas! an army without officers! How Stanley, if the Whigs at the end of the season play him a trick is to form a Government — find at least seven Cabinet Ministers in the Commons, and about five-and-thirty other officials there — surpasses imagination." And in 1853, when he was engaged in founding the *Press,* a visitor found him lamenting that the Tories were "a great mass, but destitute of ideas. . . ." It was not a very flattering assessment.

Furthermore, the society of Disraeli's own county of Buckinghamshire, and his relations with the squirearchy of which he had recently become a member, have been seriously misunderstood. In September 1848 the purchase of Hughenden, in anticipation of which he had stood for the county the previous year, was finally completed. Isaac had died in January, which helped his son's financial position, and the Bentinck brothers, as a contribution to the party, put up the rest of the money to make one of its leading members a country gentleman in his own right. When Disraeli bought it, it was a plain whitewashed Georgian manor house, with a small estate of 750 acres of wooded Chiltern hill and valley land attached. Somewhat lower down the steepish hillside on which the house perched was a vicarage, and lower still, a church, of which the lord of Hughenden was the patron. At the bottom of the valley was a little stream, with some trout, which broadened into a small lake. It was, and is, a lovely and picturesque spot in its narrow Chiltern valley, with hillsides wooded in beeches and evergreens rising on either side. Save for Mrs. Disraeli's later "gothic" embellishments, it is remarkably little changed, and modern Wycombe, a mile or so down the valley, seems very far away.

Disraeli loved Hughenden, but the notion that he lived like an ordinary country gentleman, or was accepted as one, is quite untrue. Despite his affectation of velvet shooting jackets and wideawake hats, which garb he often wore on entirely inappropriate occasions, he neither shot nor preserved game. He later claimed that as a young man he had hunted, presumably the stag, in the Vale of Aylesbury; but that was long since past, if it ever occurred. He sometimes played at fishing in his little stream. But the only country sport he really enjoyed was walking, which exercise, if the accounts of his rambles over the Chilterns are accurate, he pursued with a good deal more vigor than he usually receives credit for.

Nor, though he was a loyal and hardworking member of the county bench and had been a Deputy Lieutenant since 1845, was he on intimate terms with any of the county families. He wrote to the younger Stanley in 1858, when he was for the second time Chancellor of the Exchequer, of the Drakes of Amersham that "after thirty years of scorn and sullenness they have melted before time and events." So would others, but, though he was honored as leader of the party, there is little indication that he was loved. His only close friends in the county, the Rothschilds, were neither Tories nor, in the usual sense of the word, country gentlemen.

The usual story is that the Rothschilds succeeded in Buckinghamshire by outgentrying the gentry. Much is made of their broad acres and their staghounds, and it is assumed that by these, the usual means, they rose to social and political power and influence. Aside from being a grossly oversimplified version of the usual means, it was not primarily the way the Rothschilds gained their place in local society. No one mistook their elegant and exotic mansions (a "hunting palace," Disraeli called Mentmore) for the ordinary residences of country gentlemen, nor were their inhabitants readily accepted as such. When, in the early 1850s, the Rothschilds associated themselves with the more radical wing of the party in Aylesbury, the Liberal grandees responded not only with outrage, but with an anti-Semitism they did not even bother to veil. They would not, Lord Carrington said, "be the votaries of democracy or Judaism"; and his nickname for the Rothschilds was "the red sea." Acton Tindal wrote, with even more questionable taste, to the Liberal Whip, Sir William Hayter, who was counseling accommodation, that he would not "hand over our party to inevitable *circumcision*."

The primary explanation of the Rothschilds's success in Aylesbury politics was not their property, or their country pursuits, but their principles. Their firm and unyielding advocacy of the ending of all distinctions founded on religious beliefs attracted the support of the hard core of Aylesbury Liberalism, the Dissenters. It was, therefore, not Baron Lionel coursing the Vale behind his staghounds, but Baron Lionel demanding his rights with quiet dignity at the table of the House of Commons that struck the imagination of the rank and file of the Liberal party in Aylesbury. Rothschild money undoubtedly helped, Rothschild tenants did no harm, but it was Rothschild principles that lay at the basis of their success.

Disraeli's intimacy with the Rothschilds was, therefore, not somehow part of the proof of his integration into county society. They, and he, had an uphill fight. And, while Disraeli did not suffer from the same overt anti-Semitism the Rothschilds did, it was probably not far in the background. He was never particularly popular in the county; and it was not until his last election, the national triumph of 1874, that he finally came in at the head of the poll. Like the Rothschilds, he succeeded in Bucks, if not for the principles he held, at least for the principles he was thought to hold. As has been said, he was supported as the leader of the party, a party which was supposed to be the special advocate of agriculture and agriculturalists. Had his constituents known what he had in mind in the next few years, they would have been bitterly disappointed.

FIVE

In Search of a Policy

In October 1850 Disraeli wrote to Lord John Manners that he was "greatly engaged in endeavouring to prepare some great measure, or rather scheme of policy, which may set us on our legs, but the labor is great, for the task is most difficult." The search for a great measure or a scheme of policy was to be his great preoccupation throughout the decade. He was not to be successful. The would-be great measures never became so, and the policy never emerged. That it was a difficult task is true, but the difficulties were in large part of Disraeli's own making.

The general election of 1847 returned about 325 Ministerialists of all shades to about 330 Conservatives, of whom perhaps 100 at the outside were followers of Peel. Russell's government was dependent on Peelite support for its survival. But its existence was also considerably complicated by the fact that its own followers were a motley array. Some thirty or forty were Irish members, who had their own distinct interests; and of what we can now begin to call the Liberal party proper, perhaps half were of the Radical, as opposed to the Whig (or more precisely, conservative) per-

suasion. Disraeli gave a vivid picture of the results in sum-
ming up the 1848 session:

> . . . We have a Cabinet who, in preparing their measures,
> have no conviction those measures will be carried. The success
> of their measures in this House depends on a variety of small
> parties, who, in their aggregate, exceed in number and influ-
> ence the party of the Ministers. The temper of one leader has
> to be watched — the indication of the opinion of another has
> to be observed — the disposition of a third has to be suited;
> so that a measure is so altered, remoulded, remodelled,
> patched, cobbled, painted, veneered, and varnished, that, at
> last, no trace is left of the original scope and scheme; or it is
> withdrawn in disgust by its originators, after having been
> subjected to prolonged and elaborate discussions in this
> House. . . .

This was to be an accurate picture of much attempted legislation, not least that which he attempted himself, in the
years that followed.

If Disraeli accurately described the problem, he also
knew the solution: "Sir, I trace all this evil to the disorganisation of party. . . . I say, you can have no parliamentary
government if you have no party government. . . ." Party
government was undoubtedly the answer; the difficulty was
to bring it about. For party government necessitates one
party having a majority, and that was not easy to accomplish. Probably the party that had the largest solid core
from which to build were Disraeli's own Protectionists. Unfortunately, however, the foundation which they could have
provided was one on which no one else wanted to build.
The principles that gave the party its unity were agricultural protection and religious intolerance. No one else
wanted protection, and few wanted religious intolerance in
the precise form in which the party offered it.

Disraeli was well aware from the beginning that these
essentially negative principles, particularly protection,
would not by themselves serve his purpose of putting the

party on its legs. But who was responsible for providing the party with these principles, or more accurately for separating their advocates into a party? Clearly a large part of the responsibility must rest on the shoulders of the man who was the most eloquent and outspoken critic of the religious and commercial policies of Sir Robert Peel, the man who had led the fight against the Maynooth Grant and the repeal of the Corn Laws. It had been relatively easy to lead the pack to the kill. It was to be extremely difficult, however, to get them back under control, not least because on the protection question at any rate Disraeli was determined that they should now run against all their previous training and instincts.

In 1860 Disraeli boasted that "I found the Tory party in the House of Commons, when I acceded to its chief management, in a state of great depression and disorganisation." But, he went on, "I withdrew the . . . party gradually from the hopeless question of Protection, rallied all those members who were connected either personally or by their constituencies with the land, and finally brought the state of parties in the House of Commons nearly to a tie." All this sounded well enough in 1860, when protection had for some time been a dead issue with all parties. The situation was very different, however, when Disraeli began his efforts a decade earlier; and, while no one could question his highly realistic judgment that protection was a hopeless issue, one can certainly question both the judgment and propriety of his trying so speedily to disembarrass himself of it. His actions did little to stabilize his own party, and much to further poison the political atmosphere.

He largely skated round the issue of protection in the 1849 session. It is true that in his speech moving an amendment to the Address he argued that the new commercial system had been tried and found wanting. But he spent little time on the question, and much more on matters of foreign policy and defense. In March when he moved for relief to the agricultural interest he concentrated on what would hereafter be his main proposed alternative to protection, lessening the burden of taxation on the land. He quite rightly contended that, because the national systems of poor relief, highways, and justice, for example, were wholly or largely supported by local rates, and the Church by tithes as well as rates, a disproportionate burden fell on that favorite object of taxation, the land. He therefore argued that the burdens ought to be equalized, by a reform of taxation and by putting more responsibility on the national government for providing funds. His efforts, though unsuccessful, were highly praised both by farmers' meetings and by his colleagues in the House. The congratulations, he told his sister, "far exceeded the good old days, even when I turned out Peel."

Yet, if he wanted to forget the protection issue which he had used to such good advantage in breaking Peel, others did not. The bad times of 1848 and 1849 had revived the Protectionist cry and brought out the formation of a national Protectionist Society. To counter their efforts, Disraeli attempted in the autumn to launch from Bucks a movement for his own favorite scheme of equalizing the burdens of taxation. When the Protectionist Society protested these diversionary tactics, he responded with a letter sharply rapping them on the knuckles and instructing them in the facts of political life. This brought a protest from Stanley:

> But I confess that what gives me the most uneasiness about your letter is the indication which I fear I see in it, of your not only considering a return to Protection hopeless, but of your wishing to impress on our friends the conviction that it is so. . . . Our hold on the public mind is our adherence to the principles for which we have contended; and I think we commit a great error, and insure the loss of nine-tenths of the support we have, if we abandon the cause as hopeless, before our friends are prepared so to consider it.

Disraeli had taught his followers the value of principles, and they were not willing to forget the lesson as soon as he was. Hoist on his own petard, he had to spend a good deal of the rest of the autumn visiting and speechifying around the country to get himself out of the "scrape," as he described it to his wife.

But, though to his own party he reaffirmed his belief in protection, to everyone else he denied it. He told his old friend James Clay, now a Liberal M.P., that "protection is not only dead, but damned." Early in 1851 John Bright, the great free trader and Radical, was treated to similar information. And he had the same views conveyed through his friend Lord Londonderry to Peel's trusted lieutenant Sir James Graham, suggesting that the time had come for all former Conservatives to unite once again, with Graham leading in the Commons. Graham responded drily: "The public good will be promoted if the leaders of the Opposition act steadily and boldly in conformity with these convictions. As yet they are entertained in secret, and the measures taken in public seem to be at variance with them."

The idea of a reunion with the Peelites, though without Peel, was not a new one. The previous May Disraeli had written lightheartedly to Sarah: "If the distress continues after the next harvest, Graham and Co. must give up progress, and swallow a little moderate reaction; if it abate, we cannot pretend to disturb *un fait accompli*." Either way, reunion would come about. Yet, if he was willing to consider re-allying himself with the Peelites, he had shown, and would show again, that he was equally willing to ally with the Whigs, or the Radicals, or practically anyone who could hold out a promise of power. Disraeli was busily searching for some expedient, whether of men or measures.

His initial line of attack in the 1850 session was similar to that of the previous year in that, though careful to affirm his own belief in protection, he argued that its cause was impossible in the existing Parliament and that he would therefore concentrate his efforts on equalizing burdens, in this instance by revising the Poor Laws. His arguments showed his usual wit and resource. Free traders, he said, were against all taxes on raw materials as impediments to productivity. By their own arguments, then, they should oppose taxing the land. Whether it was the brilliance of his argument or the justness of his cause that did it, Disraeli scored a great success. Some twenty Whigs, and as many Peelites, including Gladstone, joined the Protectionists, with the result that the government's majority slumped to twenty-one, 273 against 252. Disraeli's importance to this result was underlined by the fact that not long after the triumph on 21 February he fell ill, and the party floundered impotently without him for the month or more before the Easter recess. William Beresford, the Chief Whip and no warm friend, lamented to him: "Never was there so unfavourable a state for a party to find itself in as ours for the last ten days before the Recess. No Leader whatever: I was left quite alone and unsupported." The party might not love Disraeli, but it was not easy to do without him.

He returned after Easter full of energy and new resources. The government was in difficulty, particularly over its financial measures. Disraeli allowed them no quarter; his, he said, was the party of economy; and he followed economy down, for the leader of his party at any rate, some strange paths. Radicals, including Disraeli himself in his Radical days, had long inveighed against duties on paper as "taxes on knowledge," since they raised the cost of newspapers and other means of educating the public. Conservatives had long supported those duties for fear of the ways in which the public might be educated. But now Disraeli took a different tack, thereby creating confusion in the opposing ranks. As he wrote to Sarah:

> The Radicals so frightened at what they have almost unwittingly done [i.e., turned out the government], that Tuesday night, the moment I announced my intention to support the repeal of the excise on paper, they fled the House in confusion or voted with the Government. By these means the di-

vision was not good; but their tactics have had this among other effects: destroyed the Radicals' monopoly of Liberal propositions. . . .

This was to continue to be one of his aims, to give his party a liberal and progressive image.

Such tactics looked to the existing system in politics, but Disraeli also looked beyond it. In January, in anticipation of a promised further installment of parliamentary reform from Lord John Russell, he had warned Stanley that they must be careful in taking a "position on a question which will probably be the key to future power." Nothing came of reform in this session, as will be seen; but Disraeli continued an old policy of looking after some of those who might form part of a future constituency. In 1847 he and the Protectionists had helped to carry what was supposed to have been a Ten Hours Bill. Because, however, its supporters had operated on the convenient fiction that they were aiming only to limit the hours of women and children (convenient because it was held to be unnecessary and pernicious to limit the hours of adult males), the law had been evaded by shifts of women and children working in the necessary supporting roles, while the men worked much longer hours. In 1850 Disraeli gave his support to a measure aimed at stopping the loopholes in the law, and opposed a government-imposed compromise of ten and a half hours. In this, his first speech on the subject, his rhetoric was worthy of *Sybil:* "The voice of outraged faith is no respecter of persons. Its cry cannot be stifled; it will penetrate the Senate and reach the Throne. . . . The most important elements of government are its moral influences."

Unfortunately, he did not apply the same criteria to another measure of social legislation, a bill to provide for government inspection of coal mines. Powerful friends and supporters were owners of collieries, and Disraeli did his best to defeat the measure, unsuccessfully as it turned out. As he frankly explained to Londonderry: "My friends, who are philanthropists, could not with consistency, after the ten hours affair, oppose it, and to my surprise the political economists were also in its favor." As for himself, he was never one to let consistency, or even genuine sympathy, stand in the way of political advantage.

Such a harsh judgment may seem unfair. Most politicians, after all, are guilty of occasional little lapses, for similar reasons. But in such matters questions of degree are critical; and, far from being occasional and little, Disraeli's lapses were extraordinarily frequent, and often on questions that lay at the very basis of contemporary politics. One such question was religion. It is difficult today (unless perhaps one happens to be Irish) to comprehend the importance of religion in mid-nineteenth-century English politics. Yet throughout the century it was probably the single most important factor dividing men into political camps; and there can be no doubt at all that, after the passing of the protection issue, it was the most important issue — or rather set of issues — of the fifties and early sixties. Disraeli was keenly aware of the importance of the religious factor in politics. As he wrote to Lady Londonderry in April: "Here [London] we have only two subjects, and both gloomy ones — Religion and Rents. Schisms in the Church and the ruin of landed proprietors are our only themes. The Church question has scarcely commenced, and may, before a very short time, effect some startling consequences. It pervades all classes — literally from the palace to the cottage." Disraeli was quite right about the universal appeal of the question. He was also right that it would soon effect some startling consequences, though even he could never have predicted how bizarre they would be. Nevertheless, with a quite extraordinary cynicism, he showed himself prepared to seize whatever political advantage they might afford.

In most people's eyes, by far the most important schism in the Church was one that had its origins in the Oxford

Movement. As has been seen, the exponents of the movement had stressed the continuity of the English church. But in stressing its continuity they also inevitably stressed its catholicity, its being only part of a broader universal Church. From here it was not a long step to Rome, and some, of whom John Henry Newman is probably the best known, had already taken that step. The continuing occurrence of events similar to those that had originally sparked the Oxford Movement drove others in the same direction. One such Disraeli had gone on to describe to Lady Londonderry in the letter quoted above, the famous decision of the Privy Council in the Gorham case overriding the Bishop of Exeter in his refusal to institute a clergyman on the grounds of his heretical opinions on baptism. Such Erastianism was more than another future Cardinal could bear, and Henry Manning followed Newman.

Most of those who were sympathetic to the views of Newman and Manning, however, did not follow them into Roman Catholicism. Nicknamed by their enemies the "Puseyites" for Edward Pusey, like Newman a founder of the Oxford Movement but one who remained loyal to Anglicanism, they stayed within the Church. Their position, however, was not a comfortable one. The defection of their friends was taken as proof of their own treason. As often happens in such cases, not only was loyalty unjustly doubted, but numbers were greatly exaggerated, and in the public mind they came to constitute a frightful danger to good English Protestantism. The process was a good deal hastened by two most unlikely champions of such a cause, the Pope and Lord John Russell. Late in the autumn of 1850 the Pope announced his intention of reestablishing a territorial hierarchy in England — which had, of course, not existed since the Reformation — created an English Cardinal, and announced to the world that "Catholic England had been restored to its orbit in the ecclesiastical firmament."

Russell's part, and the effect, were described by Disraeli
with fine sardonic wit in *Endymion:*

> The Ministry was weak and nearly worn out, and its chief, in-
> fluenced partly by noble and historical sentiment, partly by
> a conviction that he had a fine occasion to rally the confidence
> of the country round himself and his friends, and to restore
> the repute of his political connection, thought fit, without
> consulting his colleagues, to publish a manifesto, denouncing
> the aggression of the Pope upon our Protestantism as insolent
> and insidious, and as expressing a pretension of supremacy
> over the realm of England which made the Minister indig-
> nant.
>
> A confused public wanted to be led, and now they were led.
> They sprang to their feet like an armed man. The Corpora-
> tion of London, the Universities of Oxford and Cambridge,
> had audiences of the Queen; the counties met, the munic-
> ipalities memorialised; before the first of January there had
> been held nearly seven thousand public meetings, asserting
> the supremacy of the Queen, and calling on Her Majesty's
> Government to vindicate it by stringent measures.

The manifesto referred to was a published letter from Russell to the Bishop of Durham in which the Prime Minister,
besides denouncing the so-called papal aggression, fulmi-
nated against Puseyism as "a danger within the gates"
which disturbed him even more.

Russell, a skeptical Whig and a thoroughgoing Erastian,
was genuinely repelled by the pretensions of Rome and of
High Churchmen. But that can hardly excuse his confusing
Cardinal Wiseman with the Armada, and stirring up the
public as he did. It was not an edifying role for the great
champion of religious liberty. Yet, bad though it was, Russell's position was a good deal more defensible than Disraeli's. The latter wrote to his sister that "I had no idea of
Lord John's riding the high Protestant horse, and making
the poor devils of Puseyites the scapegoats. . . ." Publicly,
however, he not only leapt on the bandwagon, but tried to
push Russell off. Russell's letter was published on 7 No-

vember. Just two days later a letter from Disraeli to the
Lord Lieutenant of Buckinghamshire, calling for a county
meeting to denounce papal aggression and accusing the
Whigs of having encouraged it by dealing with the Irish
hierarchy, was published in *The Times*.

It is pleasant to record that Lord Carrington treated the
call for a meeting with the cold contempt it deserved and
that only fourteen people appeared at the County Hall in
Aylesbury. On this occasion, at any rate, the men of Buckinghamshire did not justify Disraeli's amused comment to
Londonderry that "the people are very much alarmed in
this country. Even the peasants think they are going to be
burned alive and taken up to Smithfield instead of their
pigs." But contemptuous though he was of the issue in
private, Disraeli was determined to exploit it to the full.
He could see nothing but advantage in it for his party. As
he wrote to Stanley:

> What will the Government do? If after the Downing Street
> Bull [i.e., Russell's letter] they do nothing, in deference to the
> Romans, then the Protestant cry . . . will gather to us, and
> we will not let it dissolve; if they act against the Pope . . .
> the Roman Members will take the earliest opportunity, prob-
> ably by a vote in favor of the land, to which they are always
> predisposed, to embarrass the Government.

A Protestant reaction or an Irish Catholic reaction, it made
no difference to Disraeli on which he rode into power. And
in happy anticipation of that event he spent the next
couple of months in evenhanded negotiations, with the
Peelite Graham, on the one hand, and the Whig Palmerston, on the other.

The 1851 session was to bring Disraeli's party successes,
if not quite of the magnitude he hoped. He began the
session with sharp attacks on the government's religious
and agricultural policies. All that emerged from the heat
and frenzy of the papal aggression agitation was Russell's
Ecclesiastical Titles Bill, which merely forbade the assumption by Roman Catholics of territorial titles and estab-

lished various relatively mild penalties for so doing. Disraeli gave the bill his contemptuous support — contemptuous on the ground that it did not go far enough. He did not suggest how far it ought to have gone. His was merely an exercise in out-Protestanting Russell and keeping Protestant bigotry where it belonged, in his own party.

On his motion on agricultural distress, Disraeli scored a striking moral victory. The motion took the form of simply laying down that it was the duty of the government to take speedy measures to deal with the agricultural distress which they themselves fully acknowledged to exist. The government's majority was only fourteen, 281 against 267. As Disraeli had anticipated, divisiveness in the government's own ranks, which had been exacerbated by the Durham letter, was pulling apart its basis of support.

In February it became completely unhinged. In the previous July, Peter Locke King, a Radical M.P., had made a motion for the equalization of the county and borough franchise. On 20 February he repeated his motion. The demand, which would have added large numbers to the county electorates, had long been a Radical object. But Russell, the prime architect of the 1832 Reform Act, had uniformly opposed any changes in it, contending that it was intended to be final, and earning thereby the nickname "Finality Jack." He opposed both of Locke King's motions, though on the latter occasion he took the opportunity to drop his stand for finality and to promise a measure of his own the next session. Disraeli had supported Russell's efforts in 1850, though he had been careful to close no options, and had gone so far as to say that he would have had no dread of the country going Radical if universal suffrage were adopted the next day. Even with Disraeli's support the government had had a closer than comfortable run, the final vote being 159 to 100. Now in 1851 Disraeli and most of his followers held aloof, and the government was beaten by 100 to 54. This ignominious defeat was too much for Russell, and he resigned.

What followed demonstrated the depths of chaos into which politics had fallen. The Queen sent for Stanley, who demurred on grounds noticed more than once by Disraeli that he simply did not have the available talent to form a government. He advised a coalition of Whigs and Peelites, with himself only a last resort. The Peelites, however, though their leader had died the previous June, were unwilling to enter into any arrangement with the man who had launched the papal aggression scare. Stanley was then called upon once again. He in turn approached the Peelites, proposing that protection should be an open question until after a general election. They would not hear of that, so Stanley was thrown back on his own resources. Limited enough to begin with, these were further depleted by the timidity of some possible candidates. Finally on 28 February, at a meeting that was evidently scraping the bottom of the barrel, Stanley finally exclaimed, "Pshaw! These are not names I can put before the Queen," and departed forthwith to resign his commission to form a government. As Disraeli later said, the government had resigned, Stanley had declined, and "it was necessary to extricate the Court, and everybody else, from an embarrassing and almost absurd position. . . ." Having turned to everyone else, the Queen finally turned to the old Duke of Wellington, who advised her that the only thing to do was to bring back Russell, and that is what happened.

Disraeli, who was furious and deeply depressed at having the cup of office dashed from his lips, later said that for him, as a result of this experience: "One thing was established — that every public man of experience and influence, however slight, had declined to act under Lord Derby [as Stanley became the following June] unless the principle of Protection were unequivocally renounced." His actions at the time bear him out, for he spent much of the rest of the session trying to slough off the issue. As Russell remarked, Disraeli's supporters were always getting up and saying, "After all, our real object is the restoration of Protection."

Then Disraeli would rise and say: "Don't take them at their word; whatever you may have heard, I did not hear it."

In the autumn he took advantage of a good harvest and returning agricultural prosperity to be even franker about his views at two agricultural meetings in Bucks. Protection, he told the farmers, was a fine principle, and they should adhere to it — so long as they did nothing about it. "Protection to a particular class, irrespective of all other classes is out of the question," and "all other classes almost are announcing to us that they are profiting" by free trade. The farmers should therefore concentrate their attention on things they could achieve, such as his proposals for equalizing the burdens of taxation and other ameliorative measures. The message was clear enough, and at the end of the Aylesbury meeting one leading farmer asked whether "protection" was a word that ought to be blotted out of the language.

Derby, as Stanley now was and shall be called henceforward, continued to argue that Disraeli's stand was contrary both to principle and expediency. There was considerable grumbling in the country. Even the loyal Sarah wrote from the depths of Hertfordshire: "One thing everybody is certain of, and that is that whoever puts himself at this moment courageously at the head of the Protectionists must be Prime Minister two years hence. You are throwing it away." There was discontent within the parliamentary party as well, Granby taking the occasion to resign from what had long been a completely theoretical troika. But Disraeli's followers in Parliament were coming around. Better times, both economically and politically, are probably the explanation. At any rate, widespread consultations early in the new year showed that most of the leading members of the party in the House of Commons approved of Disraeli's leadership and of his not pressing for protection. Even the publication of his biography of Lord George Bentinck, which besides playing down protection also included all his controversial notions on the Jews, did not seriously disturb the general good feeling toward him. Disraeli's spirits and his hopes were also reviving. He wrote to his sister on 7 December 1851: "Affairs are very stirring. . . . There ought, I think, to be a Conservative Government."

The main topic of discussion between the leaders of the party before the next session was Russell's promised measure of parliamentary reform. Disraeli's attitude was what it is now fashionable to call pragmatic. He wrote to Derby in October:

> I think we should alike refrain from being anti-, or constructive, reformers. A vehement declaration in the first vein will gain us no strength, as the Finality School must go with us, and any concerted scheme of enfranchisement on our part must end only in distraction and discomfiture. The circumstances of the hour alone can bring a golden opportunity like the Chandos clause, and if it offer we can seize it.

In December he wrote suggesting the possible inclusion of colonial representatives in Parliament: "If feasible, it would allow us to prevent, perhaps, the increase of town or democratic power, without the odium of directly resisting its demands." He was ready with a ploy for every occasion.

Disraeli was not, however, to have to tax his ingenuity overmuch on this occasion. For before Russell's measure, introduced early in the new session, got very far, Russell was out. Again his defeat sprang from divisions within his own party, though in this case the offenders came from the conservative rather than the Radical wing. The origin of Russell's difficulties in this instance lay in a dispute with his Foreign Secretary, the ebullient Lord Palmerston. Palmerston was a Regency buck who never seemed to grow old. He had first sat in Canning's Cabinet; and the foreign policy he had pursued since 1830, when the Canningites joined the Whigs and he became Foreign Secretary for the first time, had all the flair and drama of his former chief's, combined with a good deal more genuine commitment to liberal causes abroad than Canning's had ever had. His liberal foreign policy angered many, including the Queen, and his opposition to parliamentary reform angered others, including Russell. Everyone who had ever worked with him was infuriated by his habit of conducting affairs and making critical decisions without consultation. In December 1851, in recognizing Louis Napoleon's seizure of power from the republican regime of which he was the elected President, Palmerston acted in a manner that was at once highhanded and illiberal, and Russell seized the opportunity to oust him. On 20 February 1852 Palmerston had his famous "tit for tat with John Russell," moving an amendment to Russell's Militia Bill, which, being supported by Disraeli and his party, resulted in the government's defeat by 135 to 126 votes and in Russell's resignation.

Not surprisingly, as Palmerston had no party, the Queen once again sent for Derby. Even before the message arrived, Derby, who was at Badminton, received one from Disraeli urging that Palmerston be offered a place in the government and the Leadership of the House. "Don't let me be in your way. It is everything for your Government that P. should be a member of it. His prestige in the House is very great; in the country considerable." Disraeli is usually given credit for great magnanimity in making this offer; but, though admittedly the quality is often lacking in ambitious politicians, it was eminently sensible. What he said about Palmerston was quite true, and had they been able to attract him, the party might well, as Disraeli so ardently desired, have been set on its legs. Palmerston was sixty-eight, Disraeli only forty-eight, and he may easily have felt that for such an advantage he could afford to wait as a member of a government rather than the leader of a hopeless opposition.

Though Derby took him up on his offer, no sacrifice was called for. Protection proved as much a bar to Palmerston as it had to the Peelites, who this time were not even approached. Derby had to form a government out of his own

materials, and, scant though they were, this time he managed it. Disraeli, besides being Leader of the House, was
made Chancellor of the Exchequer. He thought it was because, their official residences being side by side in Downing
Street, Derby wanted his lieutenant close at hand. But he
quite rightly protested that it was "a branch of which I
had no knowledge." Derby replied: "You know as much as
Mr. Canning did. They give you the figures." Most of the
rest of the Cabinet were as inexperienced. Only three of the
thirteen had ever held office before. None of the rest was
even a Privy Councillor. As Derby repeated the unfamiliar
names one by one to the deaf old Duke of Wellington, the
latter kept exclaiming, much to the detriment of a debate
then taking place in the Lords, "Who? Who?"; and it is
as the "Who? Who?" ministry that they have gone down
in history.

Disraeli, however, was as pleased as Punch. He must have
been delighted by Derby's comparison of him with Canning; for, after he had drummed Peel out of the true Tory
descent he had created, it was on his own shoulders that
Canning's mantle would naturally have fallen. Canning
would have had it from Pitt, with whom Disraeli compared
himself: "A gentleman without any official experience whatever, was not only placed in the Cabinet, but was absolutely
required to become leader of the House of Commons, which
had never occurred before, except in the instance of Mr.
Pitt in 1782." He could not have been happier, telling his
colleague Lord Malmesbury, the Foreign Secretary, that he
"felt just like a young girl going to her first ball."

Others besides Disraeli himself were struck by the strange
and wonderful occurrence. As his fellow novelist Thack-
eray, with whom he was not always on the best of terms,
said at the annual dinner of the Royal Literary Fund:

> Could a romance writer in after-years have a better or more
> wondrous hero than that of an individual who at twenty years
> of age wrote *Vivian Grey*, and a little while afterwards *The
> Wondrous Tale of Alroy;* who then explained to a breath-

less and listening world the great Asian mystery; who then
went into politics, faced, fought, and conquered the great political giant of those days; and who subsequently led thanes
and earls to battle, while he caused reluctant squires to carry
his lance? What a hero would that not be for some future
novelist, and what a magnificent climax for the third volume
of his story, when he led him, in his gold coat of office, to kiss
the Queen's hand as Chancellor of the Exchequer!

It was indeed an extraordinary tale, and it was not over.

The Queen wrote to her Uncle Leopold that "Mr. Disraeli (*alias* Dizzy) writes very curious reports to me of the
House of Commons proceedings — much in the style of his
books." Unfortunately in this instance, however, the author
had less control over the plot. Derby, much to Disraeli's
disgust, made noises about adhering to a protectionist policy, though, as he had suggested to the Peelites the previous
year, only after a general election had given the electors a
chance to express their opinion on the issue. Disraeli, for
his part, would only tell the electors of Bucks, at the by-
election made necessary by his assumption of office, that the
first duty of the new government must be "to provide for
the ordinary and current exigencies of the public service;
but, at no distant period, we hope, with the concurrence
of the country, to establish a policy in conformity with the
principles which in opposition we have felt it our duty to
maintain." Just what those principles had been caused
some pardonable confusion.

The confusion was not lessened by Disraeli's speech introducing the Budget at the end of April. It was generally
understood to be an interim Budget and proposed no startling changes. Rather, Disraeli treated the House to an
impartial survey, which was generally acknowledged as
demonstrating a remarkable grasp of both financial fact
and theory. It proved, said the great financier Thomas
Baring, that the new Chancellor of the Exchequer had a
mind which could grapple with anything. What troubled
some, however, was his impartiality, particularly his clear

demonstration of the country's growing prosperity under free trade policies. Derby, who listened from the gallery, heard someone remark as he left the House, "It was the eulogy of Peel by Disraeli."

Disraeli's address for the July general election was similarly strong in indicating his feelings. But they remained without Derby's public endorsement. Both men shuffled on the issue of the continuance of the Maynooth Grant, in which form the religious question boiled up at the end of the session. The government therefore entered the general election without any discernible policy. Their position improved somewhat, but not enough. Estimates of government supporters returned varied from some 290 to 310. The number of Liberals was put at about 270, with rather more than half inclining toward Radicalism. Then there were 35 or 40 Peelites, and about as many Irish Roman Catholic M.P.'s. The balance of power was clearly in the hands of the Peelites and the Irish.

A retrospective view of the history of the party since 1846, which Disraeli expressed in a letter to a new young favorite of his, Lord Henry Lennox, on the eve of his own return for Bucks is highly interesting:

> We framed an Opposition on Protection and Protestantism. When you commence your studies, and read *Coningsby* . . . you will see how I have treated those exclusive and limited principles, clearly unfitted for a great and expanding country, of various elements, like this of ours. . . . Notwithstanding all I said and did, they stuck to Protection till the country positively spat upon it. I tore away this millstone, but yielded reluctantly to the belief that the brother burthen, by a fortunate set of circumstances was to turn up trumps for us. It seems to me to have done us . . . harm. . . .

This was either extraordinary mendacity or extraordinary self-deception, probably a little of both. If he had retained the notions of *Coningsby* about protection, he had certainly managed to hide them while he destroyed Peel. That he had taken up "Protestantism" reluctantly was quite false.

His only accurate assertion was that he had embraced the latter issue in the belief that it would "turn up trumps for us."

He would so believe, and so act, more than once in the future. For the time being, however, he was motivated by a fact that was evident even in mid-July: the government would lack a majority. He was therefore anxious to attract support. To this end he discovered, and sent the English Minister to Florence to convince the Pope, that "instead of the continuance of Lord Derby's Government being a circumstance hostile to the rights and privileges of our Roman Catholic population, the existence of that Government is at this moment the only cause which prevents an eruption of feelings against Roman Catholicism, such as this century at least has not witnessed." He also took steps to deal with what was undoubtedly a crying abuse in Ireland, the almost complete helplessness of Irish tenants against their landlords. A Tenant Right Bill was introduced when the new Parliament met in November, though it did not have the desired effect of conciliating the Irish M.P.'s.

Much more critical obviously was the question of protection versus free trade, which would influence many more votes. Here too the government was determined not to lose any possible support. Derby took the earliest opportunity to announce in the Lords that they accepted the clear decision of the electorate against protection and for free trade. In the Commons there was more difficulty, some free traders being determined to make the government accept not only free trade, but the humiliation of having to repudiate all their past stands on the question. In the course of the debates, Disraeli denied that he had ever been wedded to the principle of protection, or that he had advocated a return to protection after 1846. Sidney Herbert's was a just comment on such claims. "I acquit the Chancellor of the Exchequer," Herbert said, "as far as his own convictions are concerned, of the charge of ever having been a Protectionist. I never for one moment thought he believed in the least degree in Protection. I do not accuse him of having forgotten what he said or what he believed in those years; I only accuse him of having forgotten now what he then wished it to appear that he believed."

Neither Palmerston nor the Peelite leadership, however, wished to humiliate the government on this issue. They were anxious to lay the protection question to rest, and to this end they supported a successful compromise resolution. The government was to be allowed to show what it could propose in the way of constructive new policies. This was to be the function of Disraeli's new Budget, and on its fate that of the ministry hung.

The Budget was not a success. Disraeli had bad luck in that fear of the aggressiveness of another Napoleonic regime brought large increases in defense spending, which consumed his hoped-for surplus. He then attempted to create one out of thin air. Beyond that, while accepting free trade he sought to compensate injured interests, largely by reducing taxes on consumption, including those on malt, hops, and tea. The abolition or lowering of the Malt Tax had long been a cry of the farmers, in the hope that it would increase consumption of their produce. Similar considerations applied to hops. And it was hoped that the measures would be popular as well with consumers. Unfortunately, however, what the town-dweller gained on his beer and his tea he would have more than lost in the increase in the House Tax. The Budget also included a proposal, on which Disraeli never subsequently acted but many governments have since, to distinguish between earned and unearned incomes in assessing income tax. As a whole, it was another demonstration of Disraeli's cleverness and resourcefulness. Macaulay was right that it "raised his reputation for practical ability." But he was also right in doubting that he would be able to carry it. There was much to criticize, and Gladstone and the other Peelite financial experts did not fail to do so.

Disraeli's reply was, as Gladstone himself conceded, "as a

whole . . . grand; I think the most powerful I ever heard from him." He was at the height of his wit and invective. Indeed, he rather exceeded himself in the latter, referring to Graham as one "whom I will not say I greatly respect, but rather whom I greatly regard." He dubbed another elder statesman, Henry Goulburn, "that weird Sibyl, the member for Cambridge University." These and other similar remarks brought Gladstone to his feet with an attack that may be taken as the beginning of their subsequent lifelong duel. In it he delivered the famous rebuke:

> I must tell the right hon. gentleman that whatever he has learned — and he has learned much — he has not yet learned the limits of discretion, of moderation, and of forebearance, that ought to restrain the conduct and language of every member of this House, the disregard of which is an offence in the meanest amongst us, but is of tenfold weight when committed by the Leader of the House of Commons.

Disraeli was not easily crushed; but he was beaten. Despite frantic last-minute attempts to rally support, including a midnight interview with Bright at Grosvenor Gate in the course of which Disraeli proposed forming a government with the free trade Radicals, the government was defeated on the night of 17 December, 305 to 286. They resigned immediately, and their place was taken by a coalition of those who had defeated them, Peelites and Liberals of various shades. The Peelite Lord Aberdeen was Prime Minister, with a Cabinet that included a Radical at one extreme and Palmerston at the other, five other Whigs and five other Peelites.

The differences of principle were sharp, not least between Aberdeen's relative pacifism and Palmerston's full-blooded bellicosity, differences that were soon to have disastrous consequences. Derby commented: "I am afraid that personal feeling has had much to do with this step, and that the course pursued is mainly to be attributed to the jealousy and hatred (the word is not too strong) felt by the Peelite party in the House of Commons towards Disraeli."

It is a mark of the influence and power of Disraeli's character and personality during this period that Derby was almost certainly right. There is every reason to believe Derby when he told of Aberdeen's "repeated declarations to me that there was only one subject of difference between us; that, that once removed, nothing would give him greater pleasure than again to act with me; and that happen what might, no consideration should ever induce him to join the Whigs!" And at this time a Conservative reunion would have been much more natural than the coalition that took place. This is not necessarily to say that the reunion would have lasted; for, if the besetting sin of Disraeli, and to a lesser extent of Derby, was that they catered too much to the prejudices of their followers, the great failing of the Peelites was that they did not cater to them enough, enough that is, to remain leaders of the Conservative party. Differences over religious policy, for example, would have been evident before long.

Nonetheless, the fact remains that what impeded reunion at this time was not so much obvious differences of principle as distrust and uncertainty about what the principles and policies of a party in which Disraeli took a leading part would be. Such distrust was by no means confined to the Peelites. Greville had noted earlier in the year that, though a man of obvious and great ability, he was "a perfect will-o'-the-wisp" as regarded his opinions. In November, the Prince Consort had lumped Disraeli with his and the Queen's other *bête noire*, Palmerston, in remarking on "the *laxity of political consciences* which both these gentlemen have hitherto exhibited."

So far as Disraeli was concerned, it was fair comment. He had twisted and turned in a fashion which it is extremely difficult to describe in any other way than unconscionable. And even within his own party the beneficial effects should not be overemphasized. He was right that protection was a millstone round his neck, albeit one that he himself had helped to put there; but Derby was certainly right to restrain him from attempting too soon to throw it off. This was one instance when Disraeli took insufficient account of the prejudices of his followers. Even at the end, there was probably as much to be said for Derby's view as for Disraeli's. For if the latter was right that the party could not fight the election on protection, the former was right that it could not have fought it on free trade either. Disraeli's frankness probably lost his party at least one seat to the Liberals in his own county, at Aylesbury; and had that frankness been made the uniform policy of the party there would almost certainly have been similar effects elsewhere. Ambiguity was the only course, allowing the return of many free trade Conservatives without alienating the Protectionists. Nor was it Disraeli who weaned the latter away from protection, and thus made reunion permanent. It was good times, good luck rather than good management. Disraeli's contribution, admittedly a very great one, was that he had kept a party together and active. He had yet to find it a policy.

Early in the next year, he attempted to do something about this by taking the leading part in the founding of a weekly newspaper, the *Press.* "The Tories," he told one potential contributor, "were at present a great mass, but destitute of ideas, and the *Press* was to furnish them with these. . . ." He told his old friend Henry Hope that "as the paper, though Tory, is of a very progressive and enlightened design, I can neither ask nor desire general aid from the party, and am forced therefore to appeal to private sympathy."

Perhaps his closest ally in projecting reform of the party along these lines was his leader's son Edward, now Lord Stanley. Referring to his father, the young man wrote eagerly to Disraeli in January: "The Captain does not care for office, but wishes to keep things as they are and impede 'Progress.' . . . Don't let us plunge into a reactionary course of opposition and suffer political martyrdom for a cause in which neither of us believe." Later in the same month Stanley wrote: "You cannot go ahead too fast for *one* of your followers. . . . But it will be very difficult, and require all your diplomacy, to persuade the squires to consent to any plan of Reform." Another who was thick in the plot, Malmesbury, wrote at the beginning of February: "I agree entirely with you that our party is repugnant to the urban taste, and that we should try something to recover the towns' interest, but no operation can be compared in difficulty to it. . . . I trust to your genius to give us a standard and war-cry."

Disraeli did his best. In the third issue of the *Press*, which began publication in May, he wrote of parliamentary reform that "there are two men in England who occupy intelligible positions, and only two. They are both Liberals, both Reformers, and both Lancashire men; and these are Lord Derby and Mr. Bright." But, while Bright believed in what Disraeli called American progress, based on democracy and majority rule, Derby believed in English progress, based on the national character and respect for traditional influences. Disraeli said both systems were intelligible, and though it is a highly questionable claim with regard to the latter, it is clear what sort of image he was attempting to project.

There were also more than gestures of cooperation in Parliament with Bright and the free trade Radicals, or the Manchester School, as they were called from the city that had been the earliest and greatest bastion of the movement. Late in the session, Stanley joined in efforts to block government legislation perpetuating the system of dual control, by the East India Company and the state, of the Indian subcontinent, a system to which both Disraeli and the Manchester School objected. It was also noticed that Disraeli absented himself from discussions and divisions on measures, such as the ballot, favored by the Radicals but anathema to most of his own followers. As Derby protested on

20 June: "I cannot conceal it from you that there is reported to me to be a growing fear . . . that you are gradually withdrawing yourself more and more from the Conservative portion of our supporters, and seeking alliances in quarters with which neither they nor I can recognize any bond of union."

This coquetting with the Radicals was to continue. Yet it was accompanied by a strange combination, in the *Press* and elsewhere, of on the one hand denouncing the great Whig families as selfish oligarchs, and on the other of playing on their fears of their Radical allies, and urging them to pursue the only safe course and join Derby. These invitations were at least accompanied by talk of conservative reform as the only way of preserving the interests of the great order to which they all belonged. But a position which Disraeli took the following year was purely reactionary. Religious bigotry had had its annual upsurge during the 1854 session, manifesting itself in opposition to modifying the parliamentary oaths, in motions for the inspection of Roman Catholic monasteries and nunneries, and in attacks on the Maynooth Grant. Once more Disraeli seized upon the issue: "Have we or have we not a Protestant Constitution? If we have a Protestant Constitution, what does it mean? Let Government come forward; let it declare by legislation what are the functions, what are the attributes, what is the influence, and what is the bearing of that Protestant Constitution."

The speech, as it was certainly intended to, made Disraeli a Protestant hero and he was flooded with letters and addresses. He responded to one from a Protestant Association in Lancashire that he hoped Russell, who was a member of the government and Leader of the House of Commons, would take the matter in hand as he had before:

> In that case I should extend to him the same support which I did at the time of the Papal Aggression, when he attempted to grapple with a great evil, though he was defeated in his purpose by the intrigues of the Jesuit party, whose pol-

icy was on that occasion upheld in Parliament with eminent ability and unhappy success by Lord Aberdeen, Sir James Graham, and Mr. Gladstone.

Sympathetic biographers have argued that the irony was so evident as to make the sentiments innocuous, but the irony was probably lost on his audience. Certainly his sentiments caused confusion among his friends. A puzzled Stanley wrote: "In the summer of 1852 you repeatedly told me that our chance at the elections had been ruined by our taking up high Protestant politics. I agreed with you then, as I do now. Shall we gain in 1854 by repeating the mistake of 1852?"

The fact was that Disraeli was willing to follow any policy that offered a prospect of success. While Derby argued during these years for a consistent conservative policy, supporting government when it followed such a policy and opposing only when it did not, and his son argued for a policy consistently liberal and progressive, Disraeli swung from one extreme to the other, and sometimes followed both policies at the same time. He was still searching for a successful strategy, and he was willing to seek one out wherever chance or his own fertile imagination seemed to point. Such a strategy might be liberal or reactionary, or it might be something in between, as when in 1852 he told Derby that if they devoted themselves to the reform of the complicated and outmoded administrative system, they "should then have taken possession of the only questions which really interest the country, which is progressive, but prosperous and therefore not favorable to political change. . . ." Such suggestions show Disraeli's brilliance and versatility, but like so many others it was not carried far. Other policies offered more immediate prospects of success, and that was what interested Disraeli.

His attitude to foreign policy, which was to provide most of the more dramatic issues of the next few years, was equally opportunistic. When he had first entered seriously into the discussion of foreign affairs in his speech on the consular service in 1842, he had been intent on supporting Peel and had indulged in a long retrospective impeachment of Palmerston's policy for its aggressiveness and expensiveness. The following year, however, when he was turning against Peel, he joined Palmerston in attacking the government for its failure to be sufficiently aggressive in maintaining the integrity of the Ottoman Empire. Then, after the fall of Peel when Palmerston once again became Foreign Secretary in the new Whig government, Disraeli returned to the attack of Palmerston's bellicose policy. He roundly condemned meddling in the domestic affairs of foreign countries, especially in the cause of liberalism. And he advocated a policy of peace, based mainly on a firm and steady understanding with France, a policy which Derby's government generally followed in 1852.

In opposition once again, he heaped scorn on the coalition, with its many diverse elements, and especially on its foreign policy. As he ended one great philippic early in the session: "Let Parliamentary reform, let the ballot, be open questions, if you please, let every institution in Church and State be open questions; but at least let your answer to me tonight prove that among your open questions you are not going to make an open question of the peace of Europe." The jibe was unfortunately deadly accurate. For throughout the course of 1853, while Russian designs on Turkey raised a question which all through the century constituted one of the gravest threats to peace, the ministry drifted uncertainly. Aberdeen, suspicious of the new Emperor Napoleon and his schemes, tended to be pro-Russian and hence pacific in his attitude. Palmerston, with an eye to the threat a Russian success would pose to the Mesopotamian route to India and ultimately perhaps to the security of India itself, urged strong action to counter the Russians. Lord Clarendon, the Foreign Secretary, devoted most of his time to mediating between the two, while policy drifted aimlessly. Palmerston, however, had a strong tradition, and probably before the opening of the Suez Canal very strong reason, on his side. He also had the support of a vocal public opinion. Aberdeen's efforts only prevented his country's doing enough to prevent a conflict into which it was inevitably sucked.

Disraeli was as accurate in another jibe in March of the following year on the eve of the final formal declaration of war when, after the entrance of the British and French fleets into the Black Sea had caused Russia to break off relations, they were withdrawn again. "When I heard of the return of our squadron to Constantinople, I could not help recalling the words of a great orator when he was addressing an assembly not less illustrious than this, when he said: 'O Athenians, the men who administer your affairs are men who know not how to make peace or to make war.' " The disasters in the Crimea would more than bear him out.

But Disraeli had gone on to promise the patriotic support of himself and his party for a vigorous prosecution of the war. And throughout 1854 his criticism of the government was based on their not prosecuting it vigorously enough. In December, after the futile carnage of the battles of the autumn and with the army freezing and dying before Sebastopol without adequate fuel, clothing, or supplies, his voice was one of those leading the chorus of opprobrium heaped upon the ministers. Meanwhile their internal disagreements were pulling the government apart. In the same month Palmerston resigned over Russell's insistence on pressing forward with parliamentary reform. But in January 1855, when the Radical J. A. Roebuck gave notice of a motion for an inquiry into the conduct of the war, Russell himself resigned. Thus when the vote came on the motion on 29 January, Conservatives, Russell's supporters, and Radicals trooped together into the Opposition lobby to defeat the government by 305 to 148.

"The great necessity of the country at this hour," the

Press had announced on 27 January, "is a War Cabinet, constituted with the single purpose of prosecuting hostilities with energy, of repairing past errors, of saving the remnant of our army, of sustaining the reputation of our arms, and of grappling with our foe till he confesses himself vanquished and sues for peace." What sort of administration would that be? As the paper suggested a couple of weeks later, one that included "Lord Derby, . . . Lord Palmerston, and Mr. Disraeli."

It was not to be. The Queen asked Derby to form a government, but he was in one of his reluctant phases. He argued that the government must include Palmerston, whom both public and foreign opinion demanded, and that he required the administrative talents of the Peelites as well. He followed the rather peculiar course of deputing the former to negotiate with the latter, with the result that he lost both, and gave up. There are suggestions, which Disraeli himself seems to have believed, that Derby reckoned on Palmerston's not being able to form a government, which would lead to his coming back strengthened as the only possible minister. If so, he was disappointed. After an abortive attempt by Russell, Palmerston succeeded in forming a government out of the materials of the old coalition; and, though he did not retain the Peelites for long, he managed to get along very nicely without the Conservatives.

Disraeli was furious. He wrote to Lady Londonderry on 2 February:

> I was so annoyed and worn out yesterday that I could not send you two lines to say that our chief has again bolted!
> This is the third time that, in the course of six years during which I have had the lead of the Opposition in the House of Commons, I have stormed the Treasury Benches; twice fruitlessly, and the third time with a tin kettle to my tail, which rendered the race almost hopeless. You cannot, therefore, be surprised that I am a little wearied of these barren victories, which, like Alma, Inkermann, and Balaclava, may be glorious, but are certainly nothing more.

He told his wife of Derby's explanation at a party meeting later in the month: "It met everything except the chief point — namely, that we did not accept office because we were afraid and incompetent."

Most of his followers would have shared his chagrin. But they were shocked by the policy to which he now had recourse, which was joining the Radical pacifists, such as Bright and Richard Cobden, in pressing for peace. An agitated Chief Whip reported to Derby a conversation with Disraeli in October, which adequately sums up the latter's argument:

> That a party that had shrunk from the conduct of a war . . . were bound to prepare the public mind for a statesmanlike peace; that a war Opposition and a war Ministry could not coexist; that stimulating the war, after we had shrunk from the responsibility of conducting it, degraded us to the level of the mob who will huzza Lord P. through the City on Lord Mayor's day. Nothing can save the party but representing a policy.

Derby was reflecting the feelings of the party when he protested to Disraeli that "we cannot with honour, or even with regard to party interests, constitute ourselves a peace Opposition, merely because we have a war Ministry. . . ." And it was undoubtedly good luck for Disraeli that, largely because of the domestic pressures on the French Emperor and the accession of a more accommodating new Czar, peace came in March of the following year.

Nonetheless, for the two years that intervened before Derby and Disraeli were finally to come to power again, Disraeli followed a strategy based on much the same logic. Palmerston was in office pursuing a conservative, or at any rate not a reforming, policy at home and a strong policy abroad. Disraeli therefore tried to outdo him in the former and to criticize the latter for its aggressiveness and turbulence. Thus, in 1857, when Palmerston's bullying of China brought a broad coalition of party leaders against him in the House of Commons, Disraeli joined them, challenging the Prime Minister, as a Liberal leader, to go to the country on a program of "No Reform! New Taxes! Canton Blazing! Persia Invaded!" Palmerston took him up, and, though not perhaps for precisely those reasons, won handsomely. His followers numbered some 370, in a House of 650-odd members, and Conservative numbers declined to 260.

Yet, as Disraeli was fond of saying, "there is no gambling like politics." Less than a year later, in February 1858, Palmerston was out of office. An Italian named Orsini had attempted to assassinate the French Emperor with a bomb manufactured in England. Palmerston not unreasonably took steps to strengthen the law of conspiracy. This was offensive both to liberal and to Francophobe susceptibilities, and the resulting attack, joined by Disraeli who was possessed of neither, ended in the government's defeat by a majority of nineteen. This time there was no question of Derby's not accepting the Queen's commission to form a government.

SIX

To the Top of the Greasy Pole

DURING THE GENERAL ELECTION of 1857, Disraeli had written to Derby: "Our party is now a corpse, but it appears to me that, in the present perplexed state of affairs, *a Conservative public pledged to Parliamentary Reform,* a bold and decided course might not only put us on our legs, but greatly help the country and serve the state." Whatever it might do for the country and the state, Disraeli believed at this time that it might revive the party. It was part of his policy of undercutting Palmerston, and he used his own election in Bucks to try to provide, or perhaps "saddle" is a better word, the party with the issue. Derby, however, at this point would have nothing to do with such a policy; and Disraeli's initiative came to nought.

In power, Disraeli was to have his chance. The Reform Bill of 1859 was to be the last of his attempts for some time to find that great measure or scheme of policy which would somehow magically breathe new life into the party. As such, it might seem to belong more logically to the preceding chapter. For there would be a period of some half dozen years between it and his next great bold, and this time successful, reforming stroke, when he would follow a much

different policy, one closely akin to the cautious conservatism advocated by Derby. Moreover, in 1867, unlike 1859,
the issue would be more or less forced upon him, and the
daring would lie in the way he exploited it.

What makes it convenient, however, to consider the Reform Bill of 1867 and its predecessor in the same chapter is
the connection between the two measures suggested by
Disraeli himself and argued by some of his admirers since.
By this account the 1859 bill was the first step in educating
the party to the Tory Democracy in which Disraeli is supposed always to have believed. In a limited sense there is
truth in this view. The 1859 bill was to be his most successful experiment up to this time in destroying the other
party's monopoly on what he called "Liberal propositions,"
and in getting his own party used to associating itself with
such measures. And there can be no doubt that his task in
1867 was made easier by the fact that he had identified the
Conservatives with parliamentary reform in 1859. The mistake would be in seeing either measure as connected in his
mind with a democratic or liberal objective.

Disraeli used, and he knew he used, "liberal" and "liberalism" in a confusing fashion. This was made easier by the
fact that the terms were somewhat confused. One set of
issues on which virtually all who called themselves liberal
would have agreed were those subsumed under the old
title of "civil and religious liberty." Since the agitations of
the 1820s and 1830s, however, reforms of all sorts, almost
any kind of change, had become identified with liberalism.
This was because reforms were usually pursued by those
who called themselves liberals; and because they were, they
tended toward the removal of restrictions of all kinds, or,
in the case of political reforms, toward the extension and
redistribution of political power. Disraeli successfully broke
the liberal monopoly on reform in the sense of change; but,
though he often liked to suggest that they did, his reform
proposals rarely had anything to do with liberalism in any
other sense. The Reform Bill of 1859 aimed not to redis-

tribute political power, but rather to further concentrate it in one section of the existing political nation. That of 1867 did redistribute political power, but more by chance than by design.

The Reform Bill of 1859 and other measures of the government were to be entirely of Conservative contriving. Derby went through the forms of seeking outside support, but he neither expected nor received it. He was well aware, however, that a party that went on refusing office would not long remain a party, and he was prepared to go on with the materials he had. Greville's judgment that "the first class of this Government is not worse than that of the last, and the second class is a great deal better" was fairly accurate. Some of the ancient incompetents were gone, and the new recruits were better. The thirty-two-year-old Stanley, at the Colonial Office, was first-rate.

Reform was not to be taken up in the spring of 1858. There were other pressing matters with which the government had to deal. Fortunately Napoleon III, whom Disraeli had known since the days of his London exile and with whom he retained close contacts in and out of office, was inclined to be accommodating and not press the new government. And Disraeli, who had returned to the offices he had held in the previous administration, was also successful with his April Budget, which was of the careful, conventional sort likely to appeal to the House.

A problem of much greater magnitude was India, whose future was still unsettled after the bloody mutiny of the previous year. It was also a problem that greatly appealed to Disraeli. As he had written to Sir John Pakington, while still in opposition the previous autumn: "What could be a more sure basis for public confidence, and a more glorious claim for a nation's gratitude than to restore that Empire in India which the Whigs have all but lost?" It was clearly the kind of issue that had much more genuine attraction for him than the pennypinching pacifism in which he often indulged for political purposes.

With his passion for the East, India had long fascinated Disraeli; and he showed himself capable of a sympathy and understanding of its problems, which in this instance at any rate was unequaled by any other leading politician. It was the other and more attractive side of his racism that he was highly sensitive to cultural differences. He was the first to point out that an almost total disregard for Indian culture, of which the greased cartridges, offensive to both major religions, that had sparked the mutiny were but one small example, was the most important factor behind it. And his voice and influence were uniformly in favor of mildness and clemency. He was also, as has been seen, in favor of the abolition of the dual control of India by the company and the state and the assumption of direct control by the latter, and had been the first leader of either party to advocate such a step. Palmerston's government had adopted the principle for its own measure introduced early in the session. Derby's government took it up, and had the honor of presiding over the passage of the act which was to be the basis of British rule in India thereafter. They added nothing distinctive of their own to the measure, however, and had to be guided by the sense of the House of Commons, a task at which Disraeli proved to be most adept.

The reason, of course, was that they were outnumbered by a ratio of three to two in the House; and, if this impeded them in imperial legislation, it did so even more in domestic legislation. Disraeli warned Pakington, like Stanley an advocate of liberal and progressive Toryism, on what as will be seen was a critical question: "Depend upon it, if the Angel Gabriel himself were to draw a Church Rate Bill for us it would never be accepted in this Parliament. The more Liberal our measures, the less inclined they will be to accept them. They will never permit us to poach on their manor, and we must postpone our Liberal battue until we have a Conservative majority." In fact, he was never to go after this particular kind of game — quite the contrary — but for the time being the general principle he suggested held. Though the government's first session saw the passage of several solid pieces of legislation, nothing spectacular was undertaken. Disraeli himself was responsible for a bill for the purification of the Thames by a great scheme of main drainage; though, despite his later well-publicized interest in sanitation, this probably had more to do with the extreme heat of the summer and the stench that wafted off the river than with any social theories. Another accomplishment, pleasing both to the Liberal majority and to the Conservative Leader of the House, was a compromise on the question of parliamentary oaths, allowing each House to settle the question for itself, which resulted in Rothschild at last taking his seat.

Yet Disraeli had no intention of giving up altogether claims on what he called "liberalism." In October he wrote to Stanley, who had been approached about standing in a by-election at Manchester, urging that step upon him:

> It will be the inauguration of our new, and still infant, school; a public and national announcement that the *old* Whig monopoly of liberalism is *obsolete*. No doubt what you have to say will require equal tact and wisdom, if, indeed, there be any difference in those qualities. But our position is this: we represent progress, which is essentially practical, against mere Liberal opinions, which are fruitless. We are prepared to do all which the requirements of the State and the thought and feeling of the country will sanction: anything beyond that is mere doctrinaire gossip, which we should studiously avoid.

And he concluded, "We should carry into effect our policy by elevating and enlightening Conservative sentiment, not outraging it, or mimicking mere Liberalism."

What he had in mind to fulfill all the requirements and exemplify all the virtues of the Conservative "liberalism" was a parliamentary reform bill. But liberalism and Conservatism were, for all Disraeli's rhetoric, a difficult mix; and in fact in his correspondence and discussions that autumn, he did not make much attempt to combine the two.

Rather, he sketched out a Conservative reform plan with Derby, and a liberal reform plan with Stanley.

On 25 August Derby wrote that "the keystone of the whole must be making freeholders in boroughs voters for the boroughs, and not for the counties, as at present. . . ." What Derby referred to had been a major source of Conservative complaint since the debates over the 1832 Reform Act. That act had left all those freeholders in parliamentary boroughs whose property did not qualify them for the borough franchise qualified to vote in the counties under the 40s. freehold franchise. That is to say, all borough freeholders who did not reside in or on their property, or whose property was worth more than two but less than ten pounds annual value, were qualified to vote in the counties. The result was to add a large number of what can be called, though in some cases very loosely, "urban" voters to the county constituencies. Yet whether those voters came from small or large towns, the Conservatives felt that they significantly weakened their party interest, and Derby clearly considered the matter of paramount importance. Disraeli replied the next day, suggesting the means by which Derby's object might be accomplished: "If you retain the £10 franchise in the boroughs, and extend the franchise in the counties, you will have a strong case in favor of the arrangement you mention of confining borough freeholders to borough voting. Indeed this is the only mode by which even a colorable balance could be maintained between the county and borough constituencies."* The extension of the franchise, then, was to be a ploy to accomplish the main Conservative object of purifying the counties of urban influence.

The plan worked out with Stanley, who was a frequent guest at Hughenden during August and September, had very different emphases. The main points were: (1) an identical franchise for counties and boroughs, with the

---

* Counties had always had much larger constituencies than boroughs.

former as well as the latter now to have the £10 occupier franchise; (2) new franchises based on personal property, education, etc.; (3) an optional ballot; and (4) the disfranchisement of from sixty to ninety seats. They attached most importance to the first and last points. The first was identical with Locke King's proposal, which had continued to enjoy great popularity in the House. The second was to emerge in the so-called fancy franchises. The third, by allowing each constituency to make its own choice, was an attempt to find a compromise between Radicals who insisted on the ballot being uniform and compulsory, and Tories who opposed its existence in any form. The fourth spoke to complaints of the continuing existence of small, "close" constituencies in the reformed system.

The whole had a liberal, and indeed a radical, flavor. This was undoubtedly its appeal for Stanley. But whether the proposals turned out to be liberal or radical in their effect depended on how they were worked out in detail. The popularity of Locke King's motions, for example, was based on their appeal to an anti-aristocratic radicalism, which saw them as a means of reducing landlord influence in the counties. However, it will be noted that, in this instance, the proposal fitted exactly the formula suggested by Disraeli to Derby for securing the great Conservative object of removing borough freeholders from the counties and thus strengthening the party's hold there — an object that would clearly not have been approved by the Radicals! As for the second cardinal point, disfranchisement, Disraeli had remarked to Derby in April 1857 that "the present arrangement, which leaves the balance of power in small boroughs, which are ruled by cliques of Dissenters, seems fatal to the maintenance of the present aristocratic and ecclesiastical institutions." It would, he had argued, be of great advantage to the party to carry the disfranchisement of small boroughs, accompanied by a transferral of seats to the counties. Again, this would hardly have been to the Radical taste.

Predictably enough, the bill that finally emerged from

Cabinet discussions late in 1858 and early in 1859 reflected a good deal more conservatism than liberalism or radicalism. Disraeli's proposals to Derby were incorporated in toto, by the identical franchise in counties and boroughs, and the transferral of the borough freeholders to the latter. As for redistribution, a Cabinet committee in November had proposed a bold scheme — bold for Conservative interests — of gaining seventy-three seats by disfranchisement, of which fifty-two were to go to counties and only eighteen to towns, with the remaining three to go perhaps for seats to the University of London and the Inns of Court. This proved too daring for some of the more conservative members of the Cabinet, and, at Disraeli's urging, it was finally decided to compromise on a much smaller redistribution, with fifteen seats being cleared and divided between counties and boroughs. The Cabinet would have nothing whatever to do with the ballot in any form. It did, however, adopt a number of new franchises, almost certainly of Disraeli's devising, for the boroughs. These "fancy franchises" would have conferred the vote on those with £10 in government funds, £60 in a savings bank, or a government pension of £20; on lodgers in a £20 house; and on those possessed of a university education or pursuing the profession of minister, lawyer, doctor, or schoolmaster.

Disraeli tried to calm an angry Stanley by pointing to the franchise proposals, which he called "large and important," and which, according to him, John Stuart Mill said would "annihilate the rural interest." He also told Stanley that "I want the Bill, above all, to be a Bill which we can carry." In that, at any rate, he was being perfectly frank.

He was to be disappointed. In order to succeed the measure had to have an obvious enough appeal to Conservative self-interest to assure the support of his own party, while at the same time seeming to be sufficiently liberal to attain the support of the Opposition. He was to be generally successful in the former respect. But it is not really surprising that he was unsuccessful in persuading his opponents that the thin liberal veneer was any more than that. The government was defeated on 31 March, 330 to 291, on a motion of Russell's, supported by Palmerston, attacking the removal of the urban freeholders from the counties and the failure to lower the borough franchise.

Most interesting, in the light of what was to happen in 1867, are Disraeli's comments on the latter stricture. No one paid much attention, and rightly, to his argument that among the fancy franchises, and particularly by the savings bank franchises, ways were provided for the mechanic, "whose virtue, prudence, intelligence, and frugality, entitle him to enter into the privileged pale of the constituent body of this country." These were seen, as he himself saw them in 1867, as conservative hedges. Many, however, were to remember his warning about democracy. He denied that he feared that even manhood suffrage would bring a violent or immediate overthrow of existing society. But

> if you establish a democracy, you must in due season reap the fruits of a democracy. You will in due season have great impatience of the public burdens combined in due season with great increase of the public expenditure. You will in due season reap the fruits of such united influence. You will in due season have wars entered into from passion, and not from reason; and you will in due season submit to peace ignominiously sought and ignominiously obtained, which will diminish your authority and perhaps endanger your independence. You will, in due season, with a democracy find that your property is less valuable and that your freedom is less complete.

And, commenting on what was to be the fundamental principle of the 1867 bill, he said that "it certainly would be most injudicious, not to say intolerable, when we are guarding ourselves against the predominance of a territorial aristocracy, that we should reform Parliament by securing the predominance of a household democracy."

The government dissolved, but the issue did not prove popular in the country either. In the end, they gained some twenty seats, bringing their numbers up to about 287, still far short of a majority. Before the new Parliament met in June, Disraeli pursued his usual course of approaching all and sundry for added support. Under the impression of a rather larger government gain than had in fact occurred, he told Palmerston that if he would join with twenty or thirty supporters he could control foreign policy and have a reform bill "as conservative as you please." This was at the beginning of May. At the end of May, on the eve of Parliament's opening, he was promising some leading Radicals that he would be willing to support a comprehensive plan of reform based on a £6 franchise for the boroughs, £10 for the counties, and a large disfranchisement. And he made, and kept, an agreement to state in general terms his support for this sort of measure when Parliament met. In the meantime, he had approached Gladstone; and had also done his best to sweeten relations with both English and Irish Catholics, pressing appointments of the latter on an indignant Irish administration.

Disraeli's maneuvers, however, came to nought. Just before the meeting of Parliament the Opposition had had a great meeting at Willis's Rooms, where Russell and Palmerston had buried the hatchet and agreed to serve under the other depending upon whom the Queen's choice might fall. It was also decided to move an amendment to the address that the government did not possess the confidence of the House. The great majority both of Radicals and Peelites adhered to these arrangements; and they were honored, with the result that the government was defeated, and the Queen finally had to turn to Palmerston. Gladstone, who had held aloof from the previous arrangements, agreed to join Palmerston because of their strong mutual sympathy for the liberation of Italy from Austrian domination; and, with Gladstone's adhesion, "the great Liberal party" of the next three decades was formed.

The other main source of parliamentary discontent with the Conservative government had been its foreign policy.

In the mounting crisis in 1858–1859 between Italian na-
tionalist forces led by Sardinia-Piedmont and backed by
Napoleon on the one hand, and Austria on the other, the
government was considered too pro-Austrian by an Italo-
phile Opposition. Some, including Malmesbury, the Foreign
Secretary, believed that their policy had been misunderstood; and Malmesbury charged that had Disraeli bestirred
himself and laid the relevant dispatches before Parliament
as had been promised, defeat would have been avoided.
This seems highly unlikely. For, though the government
was perhaps less pro-Austrian than it was suspected to be,
it was certainly not as pro-Italian as the Opposition, or as
a vocal and growing public opinion. As for Disraeli himself,
he was highly sympathetic to Napoleon's problems. "He is
an Emperor, and he must have an empire," as he tersely
put it. Because he did not believe that Malmesbury was sufficiently understanding, he carried on a quite improper private diplomacy behind the Foreign Secretary's back. He also
understood the ties of a revolutionary youth that bound
Napoleon to Italy. And, contrary to some assertions, he
saw perfectly the connection between his own notions of
race and the theory of nationality. He wrote to his friend
Mrs. Brydges Willyams in May 1860: "What is preparing? A
greater revolution, perhaps, in Austria, than ever occurred
in France. Then it was 'the rights of *man*'; now it is 'the
rights of *nations.*'" He went on: "Once I said, in *Coningsby,* there is nothing like Race: it comprises all truths.
The world will now comprehend that awful truth." But
liberal nationalism in the Italian mold was not an issue
that could have been easily exploited by a Conservative
leader, even had Disraeli chosen to do so, which he did not.

He kept his liberalism for domestic affairs. At a Conservative banquet at Liverpool in the autumn Disraeli
boasted that his ten years' leadership in the House of Commons had put an end to "the monopoly of Liberalism,"
which he said was a theory by which "half the public men
of England were held up as individuals incapable and un-

qualified to attempt any measures which might improve the institutions or administration of the country." As has been suggested, in the sense that he befuddled his own party, this claim was probably quite justified. Having dealt with parliamentary reform once, it would be easier to deal with it again, however different the actual measures might be.

Not everyone in the party, however, thanked him for the education they had received. In 1860 Lord Robert Cecil, the future Lord Salisbury, wrote a bitter indictment of Disraeli's leadership in the *Quarterly Review*. Commenting on the late parliamentary reform bill, he said:

> It was of a piece with a policy which had long misguided and discredited the Conservative party in the House of Commons. To crush the Whigs by combining with the Radicals was the first and last maxim of Mr. Disraeli's Parliamentary tactics. He had never led the Conservatives to victory as Sir Robert Peel had led them to victory. He had never procured the triumphant assertion of any Conservative principle, or shielded from imminent ruin any ancient institution. But he had been a successful leader to this extent, that he had made any Government while he was in Opposition, next to an impossibility. His tactics were so various, so flexible, so shameless — the net by which his combinations were gathered in was so wide — he had so admirable a knack of enticing into the same lobby a happy family of proud old Tories and foaming Radicals, martial squires jealous of their country's honour, and manufacturers who had written it off their books as an unmarketable commodity — that so long as his party backed him no Government was strong enough to hold out against his attacks. They might succeed in repelling this sally or that; but sooner or later their watchful and untiring enemy, perfectly reckless from what quarter or in what uniform he assaulted, was sure to find out the weak point at which the fortress could be scaled.

However accurate an indictment of Disraeli's leadership in the previous decade this might have been, by the time it was written it was already largely out of date. In the same speech at Liverpool in which he had preened himself on

breaking the monopoly of liberalism, he had also endorsed
a policy formulated that evening by Derby, which disclaimed any desire to secure an early overthrow of Palmerston's government and pledged a disinterested and patriotic
support so long as that government reflected the conservatism of its leader, some of its most eminent members,
and many of its followers. Disraeli was largely to honor this
undertaking for the next six years It would have been too
much to expect that he would have completely stopped his
coquetting with the Radicals, nor could he resist attempting to exploit the resentment Palmerston's pro-Italian, and
hence antipapal, foreign policy caused among Catholics.
But, by and large, he honored his commitment of supporting Palmerston against his more radical allies. Partly this
was a reaction to the kind of criticism that was bv no means
confined to his future colleague and the *Quarterly*. Partly
it was that he now saw an opportunity to build profitably
on the foundation of an ancient institution.

In February 1861 Disraeli wrote to Malmesbury: "The
fact is, in internal politics there is only one question now,
the maintenance of the Church. There can be no refraining
or false Liberalism on such a subject. They are both out of
fashion, too!" He was writing about a bill for the abolition
of Church Rates, which subject he had once hinted to Pakington might be good Conservative game in some future
"Liberal battue." Clearly he had changed his mind. He was
undoubtedly right, however, that what he called the
Church question was the great issue in domestic politics.

In a sense, the conflict of Church and Dissent was the
great question in domestic politics from the reign of
Charles II, when religious Dissent first became a recognized
fact of English society, until the beginning of this century.
For whenever the nation polarized politically, it polarized
along these lines. It happened in the late seventeenth and
early eighteenth centuries. It happened again in the late
eighteenth century. The conflict could, on occasion, be
muted by other important issues, as it was to a certain

extent over the Great Reform Act, and for a longer period by the conflict over the Corn Laws. Yet when these issues were settled the fundamental division appeared once again. This was what began to happen in the mid-1850s.

The repeal of the Test and Corporation Acts in 1828 had removed one great Dissenting grievance. Several others were left, however, and the Dissenting agitation of these questions had been an important factor in the revival of Conservatism in the mid-1830's. Then had followed the different division over Peel's economic policies, which died down after 1852. It was then that religious issues came once again to the fore. Three great conflicts between Church and Dissent embittered relations. One was competition for the education of the nation's youth, which long blocked an effective government education system and very much complicated the problems of the one introduced in 1870. Another was over the Dissenters' demand to be buried in parish churchyards by their own ministers. The third arose from the obligation of all the inhabitants of a parish to pay a rate for the upkeep of the parish church. Greatly exacerbating these issues was the Dissenters' tendency to put them under one umbrella and demand a clean sweep of all grievances by the disestablishment of the Church. This was the object of the Liberation Society, whose efforts began to intensify in the mid-1850s.

Increased Dissenting agitation was partly in response to the much-litigated efforts of the parish of Braintree to levy a Church Rate. In 1853 it was finally decided by the House of Lords in its judicial capacity that, while it was a parish's duty to keep up its church, a rate for this purpose could not be levied if a majority of the vestry was opposed. The Dissenters, however, were not satisfied with majority rule; and Sir John Trelawny began to move a series of annual motions to abolish Church Rates altogether, which in the 1850s passed the Commons fairly easily only to be thrown out by the Lords.

The question was almost certainly a good deal more important than Palmerstonian foreign policy or any other single issue in bolstering the electoral fortunes of the Dissenters' traditional Whig, Liberal, and Radical allies in the 1857 and 1859 general elections. During the 1850s, however, Disraeli responded uncertainly to the issue, and in 1859 he actually encouraged efforts at compromise. But the following year he changed his tactics and made a strong and unyielding stand against Trelawny's bill. The real question, he said, was whether or not there was to be an established Church. The majority for the measure dropped dramatically in the Commons, and the majority against it increased greatly in the Lords. Disraeli was delighted, writing to the King of the Belgians of "the appearance of a Church party in the House of Commons for the first time since 1840, and the fact of the clergy throughout the country again generally acting with the Conservatives."

It was not an advantage he intended to let slip. In December at a ruridecanal meeting in Bucks, Disraeli, in his capacity as a layman of the diocese of Oxford, delivered what for all its rural setting at Amersham was intended as a national manifesto. Setting himself against the opinion of the Committee of the House of Lords in 1859 and the unanimous opinion of the bench of Bishops, both of which recommended exemption from Church Rates for Dissenters, he urged the Church to reject all idea of compromise and to stand boldly for its rights. What was at issue, he said, was whether or not there was to be a national Church; and he argued that an institution which allowed exemptions for whole classes of citizens could not claim to be national. More than that, "the principle, if conceded and pursued, may lead to general confusion." He urged the clergy to petition, to organize Church Defence associations, and to bring every possible pressure to bear on Parliament.

"What changes there are in this world!" wrote his friend, solicitor, and staunch ally within the party organization, Philip Rose. He cited Gladstone associating with Bright, Cobden, and other leading Radicals, "and you leading the

Church party throughout the kingdom!" Derby too was astonished and disturbed. "You will forgive me," he wrote, "if I entertain a fear that you have even spoken too decidedly. . . ." But Disraeli was unrepentant about "my movement," replying that "if the Bishops will only be quiet, and not commit themselves any further on the subject, leaving the question to the country and the House of Commons, I have no fear whatever of ultimate success. . . ."

In the short run, he was right. In 1861 the House tied on Trelawny's motion, 274 being on each side, and the Speaker cast the deciding vote against. In 1862 it was defeated by one vote, and in 1863 by ten votes. Disraeli had scored a great parliamentary triumph. He was also successful during this period in blocking burial legislation. In both cases, his success was in part due to an assiduous courting of the Catholics and to backing minor legislation in their favor. "We live in times," he told a Catholic correspondent, "when Churches should act together." In view of some of his earlier pronouncements on Roman Catholicism, this might seem a rather extraordinary suggestion.

Disraeli's efforts to defend the Church and the cause of religion generally from the inroads of rationalism and, most recently, since the publication of *On the Origin of Species* in 1859, of Darwinian biology, are much better known. None is more justly famous than his performance at the great meeting at the Sheldonian Theatre at Oxford in November 1864. He arrived, resplendent in the wide-awake hat and black velvet shooting jacket of a rustic squire just passing through town, to assure the Bishop and assembled dignitaries that "man is a being born to believe. And if no Church comes forward with its title-deeds of truth, sustained by the tradition of sacred ages and by the conviction of countless generations to guide him, he will find altars and idols in his own heart and his own imagination." Having attacked the efforts of the so-called Broad Church rationalists to water down and explain away doctrine, he turned to the Evolutionists: "What is the question now placed before society with a glib assurance the most astounding? The question is this — Is man an ape or an angel? My Lord, I am on the side of the angels."

Did Disraeli really believe the faith, and the churchmanship, he preached? Disraeli's private beliefs must remain a matter of speculation, but as to his public efforts one can be a good deal more certain. A comment which the same Bishop Wilberforce of Oxford who chaired the Sheldonian meeting confided to his diary about one of those efforts applies to them all: "Clever electioneering speech to clergy and church." In 1868 when he was Prime Minister, Disraeli was tamely to submit to a motion of Gladstone's making Church Rates entirely voluntary, and thus laying the matter to rest. By then he had other fish to fry. It was a measure of his brilliance that Disraeli sensed the importance of the Church issue for his party and knew how to exploit it; but, like every other issue, it was one that he attempted to use when it was useful, and to forget when it was not. The same attitude was to be displayed prominently in the revived parliamentary reform question, which was to provide him with his great opportunity.

In 1860 he had dismissed as "unnecessary, uncalled-for, and mischievous" a bill of Russell's which bore a striking similarity to the Radical proposals he had himself endorsed in June 1859. Thereafter the issue died down for several years, and Disraeli did not make another major pronouncement until 1865. In the meantime, Gladstone had in the previous year made his famous remark that "every man who is not presumably incapacitated by some consideration of personal unfitness or of political danger is morally entitled to come within the pale of the Constitution." In fact, this suggested a good deal more radical position than Gladstone himself would have been willing to take at the time; and it was infinitely more radical than a section of his own party was willing even to contemplate. The result was to give much greater interest to the 1865 debate on a private

member's Borough Franchise Bill, which had been the occasion for Gladstone's statement the previous year. A defi-
nite anti-reform Liberal group emerged, led by Robert
Lowe, and Disraeli also delivered himself of his opinions.

They had changed greatly since 1859. Speaking of the
proposal in the bill to lower the franchise to £6, he said
that "although — I do not wish in any way to deny it —
being in the most difficult position when the Parliament
of 1859 met, being anxious to assist the Crown and the
Parliament, by proposing some moderate measure which
men on both sides might support, we did, to a certain extent, agree to some modification of the £10 franchise, yet
I confess that my present position is opposed, as it originally
was, to any course of the kind." He said that such a step
"would not secure the introduction of that particular class
which we all desire to introduce, but that it would introduce many others who are unworthy of the suffrage. . . ."
If any change were to be undertaken, he favored "the extension of the franchise, not its degradation."

> I think it is possible to increase the electoral body of the
> country, if the opportunity were favourable and the necessity
> urgent, by the introduction of voters upon principles in uni-
> son with the principles of the constitution, so that the suf-
> frage should remain a privilege, and not a right; a privilege
> to be gained by virtue, by intelligence, by industry, by in-
> tegrity, and to be exercised for the common good. And I
> think if you quit that ground, if you once admit that a man
> has a right to vote whom you cannot prove to be disqualified
> for it, you would change the character of the Constitution,
> and you would change it in a manner which will tend to
> lower the importance of this country.

The 1859 Parliament had run its course, and in the general election that followed its dissolution Disraeli appealed
to the electors of Bucks on the basis of the party's defense of
the Church, and of its attitude toward parliamentary reform. He did not exclude the possibility that they might
again take the matter up, but when they did so, it would be

"in the spirit of the English Constitution, which would absorb the best of all classes, and not fall into a democracy, which is the tyranny of one class, and that one the least enlightened." Perhaps because the Liberation Society was still more powerful than the Church Defence movement Disraeli had launched, possibly because the country was awakening to the reform issue, the Conservatives only made a very slight improvement in their position, securing about 290 seats.

Whatever the importance of parliamentary reform in the election, the cause gained an immense fillip from the death of the octogenarian Palmerston before the new Parliament met, and his replacement by Russell as Premier and Gladstone as Leader of the House of Commons. The old reformer, with the strong support of his recently converted lieutenant, decided to take up the matter and try to settle it in the next session.

When Parliament met in February 1866, Disraeli, recurring to one of his favorite phrases, said in a eulogy of Palmerston that he trusted "the time may never come when the love of fame shall cease to be the sovereign passion of our public men." It was certainly his own ruling passion, and he was on the eve of having it gratified to an extent he can scarcely have imagined at the time. But he did not make the running against the government Reform Bill, which was more moderate in every respect than proposals which he had once been willing to endorse. That was left to the dissident Liberals, or the Cave of Adullam as Bright nicknamed them in honor of the place where David once sojourned "and every one that was in distress, and every one that was in debt, and every one that was discontented, gathered themselves unto him." They numbered only some forty instead of the biblical four hundred, but with strategic support from Disraeli and his party, they were able to defeat the ministry on a critical clause, and thus overthrow it.

That was on 18 June. For a time the Queen, anxious not

to change her government at a time of crisis between Austria and Prussia which was about to erupt in Bismarck's first war for German unification, hesitated. Then the Adullamites made the rather unrealistic suggestion that both Derby and Disraeli should stand aside, and that one of their own number should become Premier. At the end of the month, however, after one or two more abortive attempts to bring in outside support, Derby finally formed another purely Conservative government. This one was a vast improvement on the two that had preceded it, and, what was particularly important for Disraeli, added three new men of great ability to back him and Stanley in the Commons: Sir Stafford Northcote, Gathorne Hardy, and Disraeli's former critic Robert Cecil, now Viscount Cranborne.

It would not be long before Cranborne would have occasion once again to be bitterly critical of his leader. But for the time being, there was uncertainty about what the government would do about reform. Disraeli, who once more became Chancellor of the Exchequer, would only say at his reelection that their past record gave them the right to deal with the question if they chose, and that if they did so it would not be on democratic, but on the conservative principles he had outlined the previous year.

The public, however, was beginning to warm in earnest to the issue; and on 23–25 July occurred the famous Hyde Park riots, when, the park having been closed to them, crowds attending a great meeting of the Reform League broke down the railings near the Marble Arch and surged over the turf and flower beds. Disraeli's own house was near the center of the disturbances, and while they continued his new young secretary, Monty Corry, was stationed at Grosvenor Gate to look after Mrs. Disraeli and report to her anxious husband at the House of Commons. With her usual courage and common sense that lady was unperturbed. "The soldiers have moved away to the Marble Arch," Corry reported on the first evening, "and Mrs. Disraeli wishes me to add that the people in general seem to be thoroughly enjoying themselves; and I really believe she sympathises with them. At any rate, I am glad to say that she is not in the least alarmed."

Her husband was perhaps somewhat more impressed by the demonstration. On 29 July he wrote to Derby suggesting that they might simply take up the Liberal measure, with some modifications: "£6 *rating* for boroughs; £20 rating for counties . . . ; the northern boroughs to be enfranchised; no disfranchisement of any kind." Since property was rated at under its annual value, the effect would have been rather more conservative than the £7 franchise in the boroughs, and much more conservative than the £14 in the counties proposed by the Liberals. But in proposing the enfranchisement of towns in the underrepresented industrial North, he went rather further than the Liberals, who had not touched the distribution question. The advantages of such a mode of proceeding, according to Disraeli, were that "you could carry this in the present House, and rapidly. It would prevent all agitation in the recess; it would cut the ground entirely from under Gladstone; and it would smash the Bath [a conservative Whig] Cabal, for there would be no dangerous question ahead." Derby, however, was not yet interested.

Disraeli himself soon lost interest. Indeed, during the late summer and autumn, when a growing agitation shifted from London to the country, the roles were entirely reversed. Then it was Derby, who was himself hard pressed by the Queen, who urged the necessity of dealing with the question, and Disraeli who was skeptical. "Observation and reflection," he wrote to Derby on 24 September, "have not yet brought me to your conclusion as to the necessity of bringing in a Bill for Parliamentary Reform. . . ." In October he came around to Derby's suggestion of moving by the less binding method of resolutions. But it was not until January 1867 that he entered fully into the feeling of urgency shared by his sovereign and his leader. It is clear, then, that far from being anxious to seize an opportunity to carry democratic reform, as has sometimes been suggested, Disraeli at this time was not only not drawn to democratic reform, but was for some time not very eager for reform of any sort.

On 3 January, however, he wrote to Derby urging the necessity of coming to an early decision on their "reform movements"; "otherwise I see anarchy ahead. There are many other great matters pressing, but this is paramount." And once he had taken the question up, Disraeli pursued it with enthusiasm. It was not, in fact, he who first proposed the magic formula, but Derby, who had written to his lieutenant on 22 December: "Of all possible hares to start, I do not know a better than the extension to household suffrage, coupled with plurality of voting." Yet, though Disraeli was not the one to start the hare, he was to follow it with an agility, boldness, and success which some in the history of parliamentary management may have equaled, but few have surpassed. He was also to follow it to places neither he nor his chief imagined when they commenced the chase.

The hare was originally intended for the benefit of the House. It was at first proposed to proceed on the lines discussed the previous autumn of trying out resolutions on Parliament before undertaking legislation; and both leaders agreed that household suffrage had great possibilities for this purpose. "Household suffrage" was, as Gladstone said, "a great phrase" — it was Gladstone's misfortune that he did not realize just how great. It was, it is true, a measure which the Conservative leaders had never contemplated before, and, as has been seen, which Disraeli had repudiated in no uncertain terms. His statements during the course of the 1867 debates that the 1858–1859 Cabinet had realized that it was the only sound basis for reform, and had rejected it only because they believed public opinion was not ready, were quite simply lies. But in 1867 both Derby and Disraeli saw the great advantage in the proposal that, while seeming to be about as far as one could go in reform, it would in fact not be necessary to go so far. Household suffrage, pure and simple, would as the phrase suggests have qualified every male householder in a parliamentary borough for the vote. This is what finally happened, but this was by no means the original plan. The original scheme was to propose the broad principle, and then to so hedge it with qualifications as to render its democratic implications nugatory.

It was a splendid strategy for winning because the leaders of the Opposition could not, and what is more important would not have wanted to, outbid them on the principle. Gladstone, for all his occasional impassioned outbursts, was as yet by no means ready for democracy. The Liberals had shown themselves willing to greatly extend the franchise, and to reach much further down in society than the Conservatives had previously been willing to do. The Liberals had also been much more anxious for the extension of the franchise in, and to, urban and industrial areas, in which kinds of places much of their strength lay. This was in large part because Dissent, the great rock on which Liberalism was built, was strong in such areas. Yet, while the Liberals were ready to reach down to the skilled artisan and the Nonconformist trade unionist, they were not anxious to plumb the unknown depths that lay below. Hence all the manipulation of the borough occupier franchise. The aim was to find a level that would assure respectability. And Gladstone, with Bright's support, would try once again, attempting to forestall Disraeli and the Conservatives with a £5 franchise. It was a terrible mistake, and one of which Disraeli took full advantage. Gladstone was left fallen on the field, while his own followers trampled over him in pursuit of his rival's "great phrase." The phrase, however, would have had no magic had Disraeli not been willing to follow wherever it might lead the House. But he was.

The original plan, hammered out in the Cabinet during the greater part of February, proposed a number of safeguards. Of these the one most stressed was the personal payment of rates. This had the dual advantage that, as many working men paid their rates along with their rent to the landlord, or compounded as it was called, large numbers would be excluded;* and personal payment could be claimed as a sign of that respectability and responsibility so valued by all parties. A residence of a year or two was also to be required. And a number of fancy franchises and plural voting were to complete the proposed hedges against democracy. As Derby wrote to Disraeli on 2 February, without safeguards they could not "propose household suffrage, which would give the working classes a majority of nearly 2:1. Even Gladstone repudiated the idea of giving them *any* majority; and our friends would not, and I think ought not, to listen to it for a moment." The Cabinet's plan was meant to prevent any such eventuality.

By this time, the situation of the resolutions had changed. A general discussion of reform had been going on in the House since Parliament had met at the beginning of the month; and the House had made it clear that it did not like the leisurely mode of proceeding by resolutions. Thus on 12 February, quite in the spirit of the resolutions scheme, but very much against its letter, Disraeli had taken it upon himself to promise the introduction of a bill. Once the question was in the House of Commons, Disraeli was, to use another of his favorite metaphors, in the saddle; and this was the first, but by no means the last, instance of the flair and bravado with which he would ride.

In the next couple of weeks, therefore, before the next discussion of the question on 25 February, his colleagues had to sketch out a plan. Of that plan, which was finally agreed to on Saturday, 23 February, the qualified household franchise described above was the central core. Cranborne, who early saw how easy it would be to strip away the safeguards and leave the bare principle, had been suspicious of the plan from the beginning. Over the weekend, he did

---

* According to Disraeli's plan 486,000 would be excluded, and only 234,000 enfranchised.

some calculations which indicated to him that, even with the safeguards, a democratic franchise would be established. Accordingly, on Monday morning he, along with Lord Carnarvon, proffered his resignation. Disraeli was awakened that morning by a note from Derby: "The enclosed, just received, is utter ruin. What on earth are we to do?"

What they did was to summon a Cabinet for two. In half an hour Derby was to describe their reform plan to a meeting of the party. At four-thirty Disraeli had to introduce and explain resolutions to the House of Commons. In ten minutes the Cabinet decided to revert to a plan discussed a week earlier in response to other conservative criticisms. It proceeded on entirely different principles, being based on a £6 rating franchise for the boroughs and £20 for the counties, with fancy franchises and a new redistribution scheme. "I am going down to the House. The ship floats; that is all," Disraeli wrote to his wife. Yet it was a calm and unperturbed, albeit somewhat unenthusiastic, Leader of the House who two hours later explained with perfect aplomb the principles and complexities of the government proposals to a chamber packed to overflowing with members and visiting dignitaries. No one could have guessed that it was a "Ten Minutes Bill." It was a great tour de force — the first of many.

The new plan did not, however, meet with great acclaim either in the House as a whole or in the party. In the latter, there was a growing surge of support for the bolder, simpler plan. This was partly because no one, save possibly for Cranborne, entirely understood the complicated calculations on which the estimates of the effects of the bill were made. It was partly because the rated householder franchise seemed a plausible conservative principle. And it was partly because the principle promised success, which was important, particularly to a small but determined group of Conservative members for boroughs. As a consequence, on 2 March the Cabinet decided to revert to their first intention, and to let their discontented colleagues go.

On 18 March the government bill, which had been carefully explained to a party meeting three days before, was introduced into the House by Disraeli. It provided for household suffrage with two years' residence, and personal rating in the boroughs. The payment of twenty shillings in direct taxes would confer an additional vote. There was also to be an educational franchise, and £50 in the funds or in a savings bank would also confer the vote. The county franchise was to be reduced from a £50 occupier to a £15 rating basis. And thirty seats were to be redistributed. But the main point was the borough franchise. Disraeli had already told Bright privately that "the working-class question was the real question, and that was the thing that demanded to be settled." He now told the House that it would be settled in a way which would not give predominance to that or any other class, and bolstered his case with elaborate statistics. He also declared emphatically that under no circumstances would the government support household suffrage pure and simple.

Yet that is precisely what occurred. To follow Disraeli's twistings and turnings in detail would be tedious and unnecessary. Quite simply, what Disraeli did was to show himself willing to take the bill as far as the House chose to take it. As there was a Liberal majority, the tendency was strongly in a liberal direction, and one by one he surrendered the safeguards so carefully devised. The government was beaten on an amendment to reduce the two years' residence to one, and Disraeli promptly accepted it. It was proposed that it was unfair that of, say, three families of equal status occupying apartments in the same house, the head of only one should rank as a householder; so it was agreed to admit the so-called lodgers down to those occupying rooms of £10 annual value. Of much greater importance was the issue of the compound householders, which involved a question at the very heart of the government's bill. Disraeli successfully defeated an amendment to enfranchise compounders, but then proceeded to accept an amendment which made compounding illegal and required every house-holder to pay his own rates! The principle was saved, but that was all. The fancy franchises and dual voting proposals went without leaving even a trace. And to top the whole the government accepted a more radical redistribution than it had originally proposed, while in the counties the franchise was lowered to £12. The sum result was to double the electorate, and to do what Disraeli and his colleagues had promised never to do — to give the working classes a major-ity in the boroughs, which represented a majority of con-stituencies.

After the event, Disraeli claimed to have been going in this direction all along. He told a meeting in Edinburgh that "I had to prepare the mind of the country, and to educate — if it be not arrogant to use such a phrase — to educate our party. It is a large party, and requires its atten-tion to be called to questions of this kind with some pres-sure. I had to prepare the mind of Parliament and the country on this question of Reform." How he had edu-cated his party, we have already seen. He went on to say of the amendment which had at one fell swoop gutted the measure of its conservative credentials: "I say that the com-pound householder bowing down, and giving up his peculiar position, and saying, 'In order to exercise the suf-frage I will pay the rate,' was the very triumph of our Bill." That, of course, was utter nonsense.

He had earlier told the House of Commons, in response to the Cassandra wails of Cranborne and Lowe: "For my part, I do not believe that the country is in danger. I think England is safe in the race of men who inhabit her. . . ." That may well have been true, for there is no indication that Disraeli had ever feared democracy. This is very differ-ent, however, from pursuing it. Pursue it, he did not. His attitude throughout is summed up in his lighthearted re-mark to Stanley, who was Foreign Secretary, in the middle of the debates: "I wish, in the interval of settling the af-fairs of Europe, you would get up an antilodger speech, or a speech on the subject either way. . . ." He did not really care which way it went so long as he won.

He did win, and it was not long before he was to gain an even greater prize. Derby was increasingly a prey to illness, and the following February he resigned and advised the Queen to send for his faithful and brilliant lieutenant. On the twenty-eighth the new Prime Minister kissed hands at Osborne. Bright noted in his diary: "A great triumph of intellect and courage and patience and unscrupulousness employed in the service of a party full of prejudices and selfishness and wanting in brains." At a great reception thrown by Mrs. Disraeli a couple of weeks later, her husband replied to congratulations: "Yes, I have climbed to the top of the greasy pole."

SEVEN

Out of Office and In Again

"I LIVE FOR POWER and the Affections," Disraeli wrote to Lady Chesterfield in 1874. During the last dozen years of his life he was to experience a good deal of both. Power, fame, and glory, all of which he valued, were to be his in abundance. And, if old affections were broken by death and the fortunes of politics, new ones would to some extent take their place.

Disraeli's first lease on power would be a short one. As so often happened in nineteenth-century British politics, the explanation of his difficulties must begin with Ireland. In 1858 the Irish Republican Brotherhood, the Fenians, a secret society devoted to Irish independence, was founded in the United States with an underground counterpart in Ireland. With the end of the American Civil War and the release of large numbers of Irish veterans, both the scale and the violence of the Fenians' activities increased. In 1866 a raid on Canada was attempted. Following the now all too familiar pattern, incidents occurred in England as well as Ireland; and in December 1867 part of the wall of a London jail where some of the Fenians were imprisoned was blown up, with the loss of twelve lives and many other casualties.

The Fenians succeeded in turning the attention of English politicians once again to Ireland, but with results that would hardly have satisfied them. Disraeli, who had once proclaimed that the only way to deal with Ireland was to tackle boldly her social and economic problems, now opted for the traditional course of pacifying the Irish by the easing of religious disabilities. With the encouragement of Archbishop, soon to be Cardinal, Manning, he proposed to charter a Roman Catholic university at Dublin.

Such a program was not difficult to outbid, and Gladstone was prepared to do so. On 16 March, less than three weeks after Disraeli became Prime Minister, Gladstone, its leader since the previous year, committed the Liberal party to the complete disestablishment and partial disendowment of the Church of Ireland. Unlike its English counterpart, that church could not claim even the nominal allegiance of more than a fraction of the Irish population; and, not surprisingly under the circumstances, its privileged position and rich endowments had long been a major source of irritation to the Catholic majority. From Gladstone's point of view, it was also a brilliant move to unite his party. For all the Liberals, from High Churchmen like himself who had come to doubt the usefulness of a state connection to a largely Dissenting rank and file who disliked all establishments on principle, enthusiastically united on the issue. With Irish support, this gave Gladstone a very comfortable majority of sixty or seventy over the Conservatives.

Disraeli was well aware of the weakness of the case of the Irish church. But both because it had been united to the English church by the Act of Union of 1801 and because it was an establishment, he was bound to oppose Gladstone's initiative. He attempted to do so, however, on the broad principles of established religion and Protestantism. He insisted on the vital importance of the union of Church and State. It meant that "authority is not to be merely political, that government is not to be merely an affair of force, but is to recognise its responsibility to the Divine Power." He went on to argue that "an intelligent age will never discard the divine right of Government. If government is not divine, it is nothing. It is a mere affair of the police office, of the tax-gatherer, of the guardroom." And returning to an old, but for the past several years discarded theme, he warned that "High Church Ritualists and the Irish followers of the Pope have been long in secret combination, and are now in open confederacy."

These arguments did not sway the Liberal majority, and the government was soundly defeated. They did not, however, resign. Reform legislation, including the Irish and Scottish bills, was not yet complete. It was therefore decided, much to the Opposition's chagrin, that the minority government should continue to serve throughout the session. Its fate was to be decided by the new electorate in a November general election. It is indicative of the priority of issues in the period that neither side looked back to parliamentary reform or forward to social reform. The new electorate, like the old, was treated to religious controversies. Disraeli and his party appealed on the grounds of churchmanship and Protestantism. But Gladstone's appeals to Dissenting interests and principles won and he more than doubled his majority. When the overwhelming result became clear, Disraeli and his colleagues set a precedent by accepting the electorate's decision without even meeting Parliament, and resigned in early December.

As a retiring Prime Minister, Disraeli might have had an earldom. But he was not yet ready to leave the House of Commons. Instead he asked for a peerage for Mrs. Disraeli. He pointed to a precedent set by Chatham and to her independent fortune capable of sustaining the honor. "Might her husband then hope that your Majesty would be graciously pleased to create her Viscountess Beaconsfield, a town with which Mr. Disraeli has been long connected and which is the nearest town to his estate in Bucks which is not yet ennobled?" The Queen was agreeable, and the new peeress delighted, glorying in the monograms and coronets

with which she was able to decorate carriages and writing
paper.

Disraeli was sixty-four, his wife seventy-six. Her oddities
had not lessened with age, and outsiders found her an altogether bizarre figure. On their triumphant visit to Edinburgh in the autumn of 1867, a Scottish observer likened
her to one of the witches in *Macbeth*. Her husband saw her
very differently. The next autumn as he journeyed alone
to wait on the Queen at Balmoral, he wrote from Perth to
"My Darling Wife": "I was greatly distressed at our separa-
tion, and when I woke this morning did not know where I
was. Nothing but the gravity of public life sustains me
under a great trial, which no one can understand except
those who live on the terms of entire affection and com-
panionship like ourselves: and, I believe, they are very few."

Their relationship had lost none of its vivacity and
sparkle. The same Scottish observer of 1867 was somewhat
astounded to be told that "we were so delighted with our
reception, Mrs. Disraeli and I, that after we got home we
actually danced a jig (or was it a hornpipe?) in our bed-
room." And it was only a little earlier in the same year, during the great Reform debates, that the pie and champagne
with which she greeted his late-night return to Grosvenor
Gate had earned her the famous compliment of being more
like a mistress than a wife. Sometimes, when the pressure
of debate did not allow him to get away, his wife's
brougham could be observed drawn up in one of the courts
at St. Stephen's while he snatched a hasty supper from the
delicacies she had brought down for him. In every way she
pampered and cared for him, removing from his shoulders
all the irksome details of life which he hated.

They had four more years together. At Hughenden,
where they loved to escape to the autumnal beauties of
the Bucks woods after a crowded session, the long rambles
over the commons had ceased. But, she in a pony carriage,
he walking slowly by her side, they still made their way
through their own plantations. They also shared the in-

creasing rounds of country house visiting, and the entertaining and being entertained in town, which the necessities of party leadership, as well as his own taste, brought them. Whether the famous story of her bearing the jamming of her finger in a carriage door without a murmur so as not to disturb her husband before an important debate be literally true or not, there is more than a grain of truth in it. There can be little doubt that during the spring and summer of 1872, when the cancer that killed her set in in earnest, she suffered the most acute agonies in order to spare her husband and do her duty as his wife. Finally she collapsed at a party on 17 July and had to be rushed home. It was not until September that she could be moved to Hughenden, and there on 15 December she died. She was buried in the churchyard, and when her coffin had been lowered into the grave, her husband, bare-headed and oblivious to the wind and rain that whipped through the little valley, stood gazing down at it for a full ten minutes before he could pull himself away.

As always with Disraeli, there was somewhat more than normal egocentricity in his sorrow. Three years after her death he was still using writing paper with deep black edging. As he wrote to Lady Bradford: "I lost one who was literally devoted to me . . . ; and when I have been on the point sometimes of terminating this emblem of my bereavement, the thought that there was no longer any being in the world to whom I was an object of concentrated feeling overcame me, and the sign remained." Her loss rent completely the fabric of his life, for he lost not only his wife but the house in Grosvenor Gate where they had lived so long together, in which she had had only a life interest. He had to move to rooms in Edwards's Hotel, and he hated it. "I hope some of my friends will take notice of me now in my misfortune," he told Malmesbury, "for I have no home, and when I tell my coachman to drive home I feel it is a mockery."

He was very much alone so far as family was concerned.

Sarah had died in 1859 and his brother James just before Mary Anne. Only Ralph, a respectable civil servant to whom he was not especially close, remained. But his friends rallied round. The Rothschilds, the family to whom despite their Liberal politics he was closest after his own, opened their doors to him. Early in 1874 he found a house to his liking, No. 2 Whitehall Gardens, overlooking the river and only a short walk from the houses of Parliament. He was now, he wrote to a friend, able to "live again like a gentleman." Despite his wife's death having deprived him of some £4,000 of income, he was not short of money. Some years earlier a wealthy Yorkshire landowner anxious to do something for the party had taken over his debts in return for a modest three percent interest, which Disraeli reckoned made some £4,000–5,000 difference in his income. That had been swelled by office, and by a handsome pension when out of office. And in 1863 the death of Mrs. Brydges Willyams, his close friend and correspondent who had introduced herself some dozen years before with a letter announcing her intention to make him her heir, left him richer by some £30,000. As sometimes happens to fortunate improvidents, his financial luck was extraordinary.

But he was richer as well by his own efforts. Hardly was he out of office than he went back to his long neglected profession of novelist. His hero is a fabulously wealthy young Scottish nobleman. Three great forces struggle for the young man's soul. Appropriately enough in view of Disraeli's recent difficulties with the Fenians and the Irish church question, they are revolutionary secret societies, the Church of Rome, and the Church of England. It is not difficult to guess who wins. Like Disraeli's early novels, however, this one is more interesting for its satire on men and on political society than for its message. In it, he paid back several old political scores with interest. Probably his most notable victim is Manning, whom he felt had misled him on the Irish university question, and who appears as the Machiavellian Cardinal Grandison. Novels by ex–Prime

Ministers were, and are, rare commodities, and *Lothair* which was published in 1870 was an immense success.

Disraeli always needed more than merely money and fame, however. He needed someone to love, admire, and care for him. The care fell largely to his secretary, whose Montagu was always affectionately shortened to "Monty" Corry. Corry was the kind of handsome, lively, aristocratically connected young man to whom Disraeli was always strongly attracted. He had first come to his attention playing the fool for some young ladies at a great country house party where they had both been guests in 1865. That evening the great man laid his hand on Corry's shoulder and announced, "I think you must be my impresario." Such he soon became, and after Mary Anne's death he took on the management of private as well as official affairs, looking after house and servants and all the details of domestic life which she had always spared her husband. James Clay had long ago remarked that Disraeli needed a "nurse." Corry became his nurse, and much more. He would die holding Corry's hand.

But Disraeli could not do without female love and admiration as well. During the spring and summer of 1873 he renewed an acquaintance with two sisters, the countesses of Chesterfield and Bradford, whom he had met long ago at Wycombe Abbey, the home of a third sister. Lady Chesterfield was in her early seventies, Lady Bradford fifty-five, so the bloom of youth had long left them. That, however, had never been a disadvantage so far as Disraeli was concerned, and he was soon indulging in the most extravagant romantic hyperbole with both. Lady Bradford was really his favorite, but she had the disadvantage of being married. So he proposed to Lady Chesterfield, who was a widow. She sensibly rejected him, but they remained on most affectionate terms. He tried to see or to write to the sisters every day, and they, particularly Lady Chesterfield, did their best to reciprocate. They never filled Mary Anne's place, but they helped to fulfill his need for a female confidante, and for female solicitude and admiration. So, as will be seen, did the Queen. The Russian Ambassador, who had more lusty tastes, sneered at the society Disraeli kept as *"toutes grand'- meres."* But his grandmothers suited Disraeli very well.

The wrench that Mary Anne's last illness and death gave to his affections coincided with a marked improvement in his political prospects. For the first three years of Gladstone's government, Disraeli, not entirely to his party's taste, indulged in a cautious and low-keyed opposition. Gladstone's great Liberal majority gave him an authority never even approached since Peel's heyday. Disraeli reckoned that, given enough rope, Gladstone would hang himself, and he was not disappointed. Gladstone came to power proclaiming that "my mission is to pacify Ireland." He tackled that problem by carrying his disestablishment scheme, and then an Irish land bill. But these measures by no means exhausted his fervor. His government also reformed the army, the universities, and the judicial system. In 1870 their Education Act established the first state education system. In 1872 they carried the ballot. They also attacked the problem of drink. It seemed that hardly an institution was left untouched by their reforming zeal.

Disraeli expected a reaction, and gave it his occasional encouragement. As he said of Gladstone's Irish policy in 1871: "Under his influence and at his instance we have legalised confiscation, consecrated sacrilege, condoned high treason; we have destroyed churches, we have shaken property to its foundation. . . ." He was also critical of what he considered the government's weak foreign policy, particularly its failure to respond to aggressive new Russian initiatives in the Near East. This latter line of criticism was doubtless especially congenial after so many years of having to take a different tack in response to Palmerston's aggressive policies.

Not till the spring of 1872, however, did Disraeli begin to take determined offensive action. Then, in two great speeches, he not only forcefully reasserted the Conservative position but suggested other alternatives that it posed to Gladstonian Liberalism. At Manchester, bolstered by two bottles of white brandy concealed in the water he sipped with increasing frequency, he spoke for three hours. He stressed the party's loyalty to the three great institutions of Monarchy, Lords, and Church. He contrasted the Liberal party's violence against established institutions. Of late this seemed to have subsided somewhat, but he warned his listeners not to be lulled into false security:

> As time advanced it was not difficult to perceive that extravagance was being substituted for energy by the Government. The unnatural stimulus was subsiding. Their paroxysms ended in prostration. Some took refuge in melancholy, and their eminent chief alternated between a menace and a sigh. As I sat opposite the Treasury Bench the Ministers reminded me of one of those marine landscapes not very unusual on the coasts of South America. You behold a range of exhausted volcanoes. Not a flame flickers on a single pallid crest. But the situation is still dangerous. There are occasional earthquakes, and ever and anon the dark rumbling of the sea.

He also talked of the government's supineness in foreign affairs, and conjured up visions of imperial might. Sandwiched in was another famous remark. The country, he said, had had enough of Liberalism and political reform, but there was much to do in the way of social reform. He suggested that there had been a mistranslation in the Vulgate Bible, and that instead of *"Vanitas, vanitatum, omnia vanitas,"* what was meant was *"Sanitas, sanitatum, omnia sanitas.* Gentlemen, it is impossible to overrate the importance of the subject. After all, the first consideration of a Minister should be the health of the people."

At a speech at the Crystal Palace in June, these themes were developed further. The Conservative party, he said, had three great objects: to maintain the country's institutions; to uphold the Empire; and to elevate the condition of the people. He had nothing new to say on the first point.

On the second, he was not very specific, but his rhetoric was stirring. He proclaimed that the working classes were Conservative in the "purest and loftiest" sense, that they "are proud of belonging to a great country, and wish to maintain its greatness — that they are proud of belonging to an Imperial country, and are resolved to maintain, if they can, their empire — that they believe on the whole that the greatness and empire of England are to be attributed to the ancient institutions of the land." On the third point, though he devoted least time to it, he was rather more specific. The subject, he said,

> involves the state of the dwellings of the people, the moral consequences of which are not less considerable than the physical. It involves their enjoyment of some of the chief elements of nature — air, light, and water. It involves the regulation of their industry, the inspection of their toil. It involves the purity of their provisions, and it touches upon all the means by which you may wean them from habits of excess and of brutality.

He was not to have the opportunity to implement any of these points for a while. In 1873, however, the fissures which had for the past couple of years been visible in Gladstone's majority opened wide. The Prime Minister proposed to do what Disraeli had failed to do, establish a Roman Catholic university in Ireland. He too failed. His measure gave the Catholic hierarchy too little power to please the Irish, and too much to please the Protestants. As a consequence, ill supported by his own party, he was beaten by a combination of Conservative and Irish votes on 12 March. Gladstone resigned, but Disraeli would not play the old game and take office while his opponents patched up their differences and prepared to throw him out. He argued that a government with a majority had been defeated by divisions within its own ranks, and he refused to take office. Gladstone was therefore forced to resume his place. He did not, however, intend to meet the same Parliament again; and early the next year he dissolved and appealed to the country with a promise to abolish the income tax.

He was soundly defeated, though it is unclear whether it was because of his being too liberal, as Disraeli had reckoned, or not liberal enough. The Dissenters had been angered by the fact that the Education Act of 1870, instead of establishing a uniform system of nonsectarian education, had continued to subsidize denominational schools, which were mainly those of the established Church. They therefore tended either to put up their own candidates and divide the Liberal vote or not to vote at all. This was very likely the main factor in the Liberal defeat, though it is undoubtedly true that there was growing alienation from Liberalism in a fast-developing suburbia, particularly around London. And Lancashire, probably mainly because of the area's large Irish Catholic population and the strong adverse feelings it engendered in the Protestant majority, was also an area of growing Conservative strength. Another factor was a vastly superior Conservative organization, particularly its development of local associations which Disraeli had strongly encouraged since 1868 and whose gatherings had occasioned his two speeches in 1872. At any rate, whatever the reason, the Conservatives won a smashing victory. Disraeli, for the first time, topped the poll in Bucks, and his party took 350 seats, to the Liberals' 245, and the new Irish Home Rule party's 57.

Gladstone resigned on 17 February, and the Queen sent for Disraeli to wait on her the next day at Windsor. He was ecstatic, telling her that "nothing like this had been anticipated, and no party organization cd. have caused this result of a majority of nearly 64. Not since the time of Pitt and Fox had there been anything like it." She was evidently delighted to see him: "He repeatedly said whatever I wished shd. be done — whatever his difficulties might be!"

The turning point in the relationship between Disraeli and the Queen can be dated from the death of the Prince

Consort in December 1861 and her appreciation of his sympathy on that tragic event. Before that neither she nor her husband, as has been seen, had liked or trusted him. The second Derby-Disraeli government improved relations somewhat, but not beyond a kind of skeptical toleration on the royal couple's part. What won her heart was the sympathy and appreciation of the Prince that Disraeli took care to express on every occasion public and private. As he said in the debate on a monument to Albert in 1863, it "should, as it were, represent the character of the Prince himself in the harmony of its proportions, in the beauty of its ornament, and in its enduring nature. It should be something direct, significant, and choice, so that those who come after us may say: 'This is the type and testimony of a sublime life and a transcendent career, and thus they were recognised by a grateful and admiring people.'" Whether the Albert Memorial achieved all this may perhaps be open to question. But the Queen was delighted with the speech, writing to express "personally, to Mr. Disraeli her deep gratification at the tribute he paid to her adored, beloved, and great husband. The perusal of it made her shed many tears, but it was very soothing to her broken heart to see such true appreciation of that spotless and unequalled character."

Besides his appreciation of the holy ghost, Disraeli's new conservative stance and restrained, and what she saw as responsible, opposition to Palmerston after 1859 favorably impressed the Queen. Anxious as she was to settle the Reform question, his flexibility and willingness to compromise in 1867 won him the highest marks. She continued to approve of his policy as her Prime Minister. And personally he was so pleasant. As one of her ladies-in-waiting wrote to a political opponent of the Prime Minister's: "Dizzy writes daily letters to the Queen in his best novel style, telling her every scrap of political news dressed up to serve his own purpose, and every scrap of social gossip cooked to amuse her. She declares that she never had such letters in her life, which is probably true, and that she never before knew *everything!*"

Not only did he charm her with his own literary style, but also by a perhaps excessive appreciation of her own. When in January 1868 she sent him a copy of her *Leaves from the Journal of our Life in the Highlands,* he wrote back to say that "its vein is innocent and vivid; happy in picture and touched with what I ever think is the characteristic of our royal mistress — grace." Hereafter, we are informed on good authority, whenever he had occasion to discuss literary subjects with the Queen, he would preface his remarks with, "We authors, Ma'am." His attentions were repaid, and it was also during this first premiership that the famous gifts of flowers began to arrive: "She heard him say one day that he was so fond of May and of all those lovely spring flowers that she has ventured to send him these, as they will make his rooms look so bright." It is hardly surprising that she missed him when he went, and that after Gladstone, who, besides his abhorrent policies, she once said addressed her like a public meeting, she was glad to have him back.

What of Disraeli? He certainly had no illusions about what he was doing. As he told Matthew Arnold in a conversation shortly before his death: "You have heard me called a flatterer, and it is true. Everyone likes flattery; and, when you come to royalty, you should lay it on with a trowel." Nor, despite all his exalted talk of monarchy in his novels and later to the Queen, did he ever believe for an instant in the existence or in the increase of significant monarchical power. In the autumn of 1866, when the Queen offered to intervene with the Opposition in order to secure a settlement of the Reform question, Disraeli wrote contemptuously to Northcote: "The royal project of gracious interposition with our rivals is a mere phantom. It pleases the vanity of a Court deprived of substantial power, but we know, from the experience of similar sentimental schemes, that there is nothing practical in it. . . ." He undoubtedly loved the ceremonial pageantry of royalty and appreciated its symbolic and psychological value, and by coaxing the Queen once more into the public eye and increasing the romance that surrounded her crown, he did a great deal to give the monarchy its modern position. That, however, was the extent of his monarchism.

Yet, particularly during the second ministry, there was something special in the relationship between Disraeli and the woman whom, in a manner reminiscent of Spenser and his celebration of her great predecessor, he came to call "the Faery." Mary Anne's death increased the bond of sympathy between them. "It is strange," he wrote to Lady Bradford about his black-edged writing paper, "but I always used to think that the Queen, persisting in these emblems of woe, indulged in a morbid sentiment; and yet it has become my lot, and seemingly an irresistible one." Disraeli turned to the Queen, as he turned to the two sisters, for comfort. There was even the same language of love, though admittedly in its more extravagant form at second hand. He wrote to one of her ladies, and certainly for her eyes, during one of their infrequent serious differences of opinion: "I love the Queen — perhaps the only person in this world left to me that I do love. . . ."

The Queen was, of course, the perfect confidante for the Prime Minister. He could pour into her ears all his hopes, and fears, and plans and be assured of an informed and interested, as well as sympathetic, audience. Stanley, or Derby as he had become on his father's death in 1869, was concerned early in the government's life that Disraeli went too far in his confidences and flattery. "Is there not," he wrote to Disraeli in May 1874, "just a risk of encouraging her in too large ideas of her personal power, and too great indifference to what the public expects?" It is a difficult question to answer even now. It was certainly hard to encourage the Queen to believe in her power and not sometimes concede to her wishes, and on a couple of occasions Disraeli got into difficulty by allowing her to push him further than he ought to have gone. On the other side, however, his arts of management made his life at least a great deal easier; furthermore, he enjoyed them.

In the General Preface to the complete edition of his novels published in 1870, Disraeli summed up what he claimed to have been his objectives since his entry into political life. Of those not yet attained, one was the restoration of a "real throne." We have just seen his views on that question. Another object was "to infuse life and vigour into the Church. . . ." We shall presently see more of his efforts toward that end. A third was "to elevate the physical as well as the moral condition of the people. . . ." It is in this area more than any other, at any rate in domestic affairs, that he is best remembered by his party and by posterity generally; and it is to this area of his activities that we shall now turn our attention.

John Gorst, the great architect of the party organization, summed up in a letter to *The Times* in 1907 what he understood to have been the domestic policy of his "ancient master":

> The principle of Tory democracy is that all government exists solely for the good of the governed; that Church and King, Lords and Commons, and all other public institutions are to be maintained so far, and so far only, as they promote the happiness and welfare of the common people; that all who are entrusted with any public function are trustees, not for their own class, but for the nation at large; and that the mass of the people may be trusted so to use electoral power, which should be freely conceded to them, as to support those who are promoting their interests. It is democratic because the welfare of the people is its supreme end; it is Tory because the institutions of the country are the means by which the end is to be attained.

The ideal of Tory Democracy has probably never been better described. That it is a myth would seem to be too evident to need elaborate justification. Yet most political ideals are in part myth, and few would deny that this has been a potent and highly beneficial one. How far does Disraeli deserve the credit for it?

He was to receive credit for such views even before he died, from H. M. Hyndman, the founder of the Social Democratic Federation, among others. He did nothing to discourage people who believed in this way, and, as will be obvious to those who have read thus far, one could find ample justification for such a belief among his public statements. But such evidence does not, of course, provide an answer to the question; and, in fact, no simple answer is possible.

At the most obvious level, it is evident that Disraeli did not believe in the principles Gorst enunciated. As has been seen in the discussion of the 1867 Reform Act, he had no convictions about democracy. The most one can say is that he probably did not fear it, but it was never an object with him. He pursued parliamentary reform solely for its political advantage to himself and to his party, which amounted to the same thing, and that was his only interest in it. It would also be very difficult, on the basis of his career to this date, to believe that he would ever have pursued any policy which he did not conceive to be to his ultimate political advantage; and it is unnecessary to believe so. His willingness to throw over his principles when they were politically inconvenient, as for example government regulation in the case of the mines in 1850, has already been noted. Nor is there evidence that he ever acted solely from disinterested motives on other occasions. Political expediency was always his touchstone.

As it happened, however, political expediency generally coincided with a policy of at least moderate social reform. Before the 1867 Reform Act such a policy was a useful way to seek support and mobilize pressure outside the political nation, a tactic which politicians had pursued in a not dissimilar fashion at least from the days of Disraeli's hero Bolingbroke; and after further parliamentary reform became generally accepted as only a matter of time after 1850, it was a useful way to appeal to a future electorate. After 1867, of course, that electorate was no longer a thing of the future, but a present reality.

It would not do, however, to overemphasize the changes wrought by the 1867 Reform Act. Though it is true to say that in the boroughs, which constituted a majority of constituencies and returned a majority of members,* it gave the working classes a majority, one must not understand this in modern terms. A useful statistic to suggest the lack of modernity in the electorate is that of some 650 members of the House of Commons only 114 were returned from boroughs with populations of 50,000 or over. This was in 1871, and the situation it reflects would persist until the reforms of 1884–1885 established roughly equal electoral districts. By then Disraeli was dead. The political system he helped to shape and in which he was to live out the rest of his career, therefore, was one that continued to give predominance to the smaller towns and the countryside, the world of the past, rather than to the urban and industrial world of the future.

Thus the reforms in housing, sanitation, and factory regulation which Disraeli suggested in his 1872 speeches and which his government was to carry, while they would have appealed to a section of the electorate and one well worth bidding for, would probably not have had much appeal for the majority. They certainly would not have appealed to the rural and agricultural forces which remained the backbone of the Conservative party, and if pressed too far they would have alienated promising new recruits from the middle classes. Indeed it was just as well for Disraeli, and largely through his efforts, that the fears of the property-owning classes during this period were concentrated on Ireland: on Gladstone's attack on the property of the Irish church, and on his reforms of Irish land law increasingly in favor of the tenant, which interfered

---

* In England, for example, 281 members to 170 for the counties.

with freedom of contract and the landlord's control over his own property. Such fears, capable of uniting adherents of Manchester economics with their former bitter enemies the landowning aristocracy, would create a new Conservative party under his successor, Lord Salisbury. But their effects were already clearly apparent in Disraeli's day.

As Paul Smith has shown in his excellent book on the subject, Disraeli was well aware of the political realities he faced and intent on exploiting them. In large part, his response was to embrace enthusiastically a philosophy he had once reviled. As he said in justification of his Reform policy in 1867: "In a progressive country change is constant; and the great question is, not whether you should resist change which is inevitable, but whether that change should be carried out in deference to the manners, the customs, the laws, the traditions of the people, or in deference to abstract principles and arbitrary and general doctrines." Peel could not have said it better. Nor could any measure have better exemplified Taper's famous perception of sound Conservatism in *Coningsby* — "I understand: Tory men and Whig measures" — than the Reform Act carried by his creator.

Yet Disraeli was to add critical elements of his own to the Peelite Conservatism to which, by devious routes, he led his party back. In domestic affairs two were of the first importance. One was an exploitation of religious bigotry to which Peel would never have stooped, but which would long remain a key factor in his party's appeal to those in all classes of society. The other was a policy of social reform aimed explicitly at the urban and industrial working classes. Peel had not only not desired, but had actively fought against such elements of that policy as had been broached in the 1840s. Disraeli, with a consistency which is especially remarkable in him, had been not only one of the earliest proponents, but also one of the staunchest supporters of a policy of social reform throughout his career. It is the one area of politics in which self-interested opportunism never seriously subordinated the warm and generous elements in his nature. Doubtless this was largely a matter of chance, in that his political opponents never chose to take up such a policy, Gladstone generally preferring libertarian to social reforms. But even if it was in part an accident, one can hardly doubt that it was a fortunate accident, in his own time, and even more for posterity.

It is true that Disraeli was not the architect of the social reforms that his government undertook. He had told the Queen in their first interview that "he was anxious to bring as much new talent and blood into the Govt. as possible. . . ." He was remarkably successful, and nowhere more so than in the man he made Home Secretary. Richard Cross was a Lancashire banker, and like the new Lord Derby a representative of that county's progressive Conservatism. Cross, as he later recorded, was somewhat taken aback when the leaders of the new government met to shape its policies:

> When the Cabinet came to discuss the Queen's Speech, I was, I confess, disappointed at the want of originality shown by the Prime Minister. From all his speeches, I had quite expected that his mind was full of legislative schemes, but such did not prove to be the case; on the contrary, he had to entirely rely on the various suggestions of his colleagues, and as they themselves had only just come into office, and that suddenly, there was some difficulty in framing the Queen's Speech.

This is not actually very surprising. Disraeli's main attention, as we shall see, was elsewhere, on foreign affairs. And, as we have seen, contrary to Gorst's view, social reform was never his sole domestic preoccupation, but only one among several. The fact is, however, that though Cross drew up the measures, they were, as Cross himself suggests above, largely inspired by Disraeli's earlier utterances. Even when they were not, Disraeli quickly grasped their importance; and throughout he backed Cross to the hilt. The credit

which he has received for the government's social legislation is not, therefore, really misplaced.

The most important legislation was framed in the autumn of 1874 and passed in the session of 1875. The Artisans' Dwellings Act allowed municipal authorities in the
larger towns to draw up improvement schemes for areas
certified by a medical officer to be unhealthy. The land
involved could be purchased, compulsorily if necessary, and
it was then to be let or sold for the purpose of providing
new working-class housing. Cheap government loans were
to be made available for all these purposes, though the
actual building of the new housing was to be undertaken
by private enterprise.

Two other acts aimed at improving the lot of the worker
and putting the trade unions on a firm legal foundation.
One placed employers and workmen on an equal footing
before the law in regard to labor contracts, making a
breach of contract merely a civil, instead of a criminal, of-
fense for the latter as it had always been for the former. The
other act legalized peaceful picketing and provided that a
trade union could not be punished for any act allowable
in a single individual, conceding in both respects what a
Liberal act of 1871 withheld.

In the same year Cross consolidated and improved the
whole sanitary code in one great Public Health Act, and
Disraeli himself piloted through the Commons an act giving agricultural tenants in England the same right to
compensation for unexhausted improvements as had been
conceded to Irish tenants in 1870. The previous year the
government had finally given workmen the ten-hour day
for which Disraeli had fought in 1850. In 1878 all previous
factory legislation was brought under one Consolidation
Act. In 1876 the Rivers Pollution Act absolutely prohibited
the introduction of solid matter into the rivers and made
manufacturers legally responsible for liquids flowing from
their works. Another act in the same year involved the
state in the protection of merchant seamen. Still another

prohibited any further enclosure of common land save where it would serve a public purpose, and promoted free access to the commons and their use as public playgrounds. Yet other acts of the government during the course of its existence aimed to prevent the adulteration of food and medical quackery, and gave protection to small savings in Friendly Societies.

The criticisms usually made of the social reforms of Disraeli's second government are that a great deal more might have been attempted, and that a great deal of what was attempted was rendered nugatory by the fact that much of the legislation was permissive rather than compulsory. Both criticisms are doubtless justified. As to the second, Disraeli had been opposed to compulsory centralized legislation since the days of the New Poor Law, and there were excellent political reasons for his remaining so. He said on the subject in speaking of his Agricultural Tenants Bill: "Permissive legislation is the character of a free people. It is easy to adopt compulsory legislation when you have to deal with those who only exist to obey; but in a free country, and especially in a country like England, you must trust to persuasion and example as the two great elements, if you wish to effect any great changes in the manners of the people." The effectiveness of persuasion and example can undoubtedly be overestimated, but they can also be underestimated; and it was certainly not unimportant that government should have attempted to set an example in the several areas touched on by their legislation. Furthermore, in progressive municipalities, such as Birmingham and later in the area controlled by the London County Council, immense practical good was accomplished under the government's permissive acts. There is probably no more striking tribute to the importance of the whole body of its legislation than that of Alexander Macdonald, one of the first two workingmen to be elected to Parliament, who told his constituents in 1879 that "the Conservative party have done more for the working classes in five years than the Liberals have in fifty."

As has been suggested, Disraeli was fully aware of the importance of these measures. Speaking of the Artisans' Dwellings Bill and the bill to promote and safeguard small savings, he told Lady Bradford that they were "important, because they indicate a policy round wh. the country can rally." Of the labor legislation of 1875, he told the Queen that the two bills were hailed as "a complete and satisfactory solution of the greatest question of the day; the relations between Capital and Labor." And addressing himself specifically to the one that put employer and employee on an equal legal footing:

> Mr. Disraeli believes, that this measure, settling all the long-envenomed disputes between "master and servant," is the most important of the class, that has been carried in your Majesty's long and eventful reign: more important, he thinks, because of more extensive and general application, than even the Short Time [i.e., Ten Hours] Acts, which have had so beneficial an effect in softening the feelings of the working multitude.
>
> He is glad, too, that this measure was virtually passed on your Majesty's Coronation Day. . . .

Writing to Lady Bradford on the same day, 29 June, he said that the bills were "measures that root and consolidate a party." He went on to confide what

> I will tell to no other being, not even the Faery, to whom I am now going to write a report of the memorable night, that when Secy. X explained his plan to the Cabinet, many were agst. it, and none for it but myself; and it was only in deference to the P. Min[iste]r that a decision was postponed to another day. In the interval the thing was better understood and managed.

It is because of this kind of interest and support that Disraeli deserves credit for his government's legislation. And also for the fact that his soaring rhetoric continued to endow mundane, but critical, subjects with meaning and importance; as for example, his remark at the end of the 1875 session about sanitary reform, "that phrase so little understood," but which includes "most of the civilising influences of humanity." There was the authentic voice of the author of *Sybil*.

With such sympathy and imagination, combined with undoubted brilliance, one wonders what would have happened had Disraeli devoted his powers to statesmanship. But in him the crafty and scheming politician, elements of which must admittedly be present in every statesman, outweighed the disinterested and constructive elements in his character. All politicians must compromise, but most politicians have convictions to be compromised. Disraeli did not. There was no subject too serious to serve the needs of expediency, no cause which could not be sacrificed. Nowhere is this more evident than in what to most people remained the great question of the day, religion.

It is perhaps because the urgency of religion has declined that Disraeli has enjoyed such generally kind treatment in this century. Many today can sympathize with his description to Lady Bradford of " 'schools of Church thought,' *alias* Church nonsense." And provided sectarian disputes do not impinge upon our own lives, we can look upon them with amused tolerance. Such was not the case in Disraeli's day. Throughout his career religious and sectarian disputes were at the very basis of politics. He knew it, and, with a cool detachment, he exploited and played upon them without limit or compunction.

The new government had moved cautiously toward its social reforms, passing only the act instituting the ten-hour day and appointing a Royal Commission on labor law in its first session. But it was plunged immediately into religious controversy. Disraeli had made much of the education question in his own Bucks election. As has been suggested, the Liberal Education Act of 1870, while aiming to put an elementary education within at least the physical reach of every child, had built upon an existing system of denominational, and mainly Anglican, schools. Where such schools provided adequate accommodation, the new school boards, with their nondenominational, rate-supported schools, would not be instituted. The state also continued to subsidize denominational schools directly; and the controversial twenty-fifth clause of the Education Act, which allowed school boards to pay the still required school fees for children whose parents could not afford them, also allowed the parents to use those fees at a denominational school if they chose. It was the continued subsidization of denominational education that so angered the Dissenters in the election. Predictably enough, Disraeli saw the continuance, and if possible extension, of state support to denominational schools as a critical electoral gambit of the Church party; and his government pursued this object throughout. Even their institution of compulsory education in 1876 was in large part motivated by a desire to assist Church schools by pumping more fees into them.

It was not, however, the education question, but what Gladstone called, and Disraeli agreed to be, a bill "to put down Ritualism" that was to occupy the center of attention in 1874. The Ritualists represented another outgrowth of the Oxford Movement, with its emphasis on the catholicity of the English Church; but, as the name suggests, the Ritualists put a major emphasis on liturgical questions, being concerned with such matters as eucharistic vestments, the eastward position by the celebrant, wafer bread, and the mixed chalice. As has been seen, Disraeli had not hesitated in the past to exploit the strong Protestant feeling against what most saw as a fifth column in the Church. This time he was more cautious.

The reason, once again, was political. As he had written to Salisbury, who had agreed to join the government as Secretary of State for India, on 22 February: "You were very right in saying, that the only obvious difficulties we should have in our Govt. would, or rather might, be religious ones." The general difficulty was that his government represented a delicate balance between Church parties. Salisbury was the leading High Churchman in the Cabinet; and, while he did not sympathize with all of what Disraeli called the "high jinks" of the Ritualists, both on principle and in the interests of the internal peace of the Church he disapproved of any interference with them. The specific difficulty which occasioned the letter was that the Queen was determined to deal a strong blow against Ritualism, and in this instance was intent on demonstrating her disapproval by excluding any of its adherents from her Household.

This difficulty was got over with Salisbury's assistance, but the introduction of a bill by the Archbishop of Canterbury, strongly backed by the Queen, proved a more difficult problem to get around. The details are not important. Suffice it to say that Disraeli, after long playing a mediating role, decided in July that the time was ripe to strike a blow for Protestantism. He therefore opposed counter resolutions by the High Church Gladstone. He agreed that the Public Worship Regulation Bill was "to put down Ritualism," and he associated himself and the government with the measure. While professing himself not opposed to differences of opinion within the Church, he was opposed to "practices by a portion of the clergy, avowedly symbolic of doctrines which the same clergy are bound, in the most solemn manner, to refute and repudiate." Disraeli was careful to avow his respect for Roman Catholics, who were now his allies on the education question. He had no objection to Roman Catholic doctrines and ceremonies, when their adherents were Roman Catholics. What he did object to was the "Mass in masquerade." And he urged, and successfully, the passage of the bill.

Disraeli's stand once again established him as the Protestant champion, as he desired. And because the bill had been amended to meet their scruples, Salisbury and his High Church colleagues remained, and the government came through intact. But High Churchmen generally were embittered, and there were unfortunate consequences for Disraeli. Gorst warned him that "the potential electoral strength of the High Church party is generally underestimated on our side. If they become actively hostile, as the Dissenters were to Gladstone before the dissolution, we should lose many seats both in the counties and boroughs." The electoral impact of their hostility is difficult to calculate, but there can be no doubt that their opposition helped greatly to complicate the conduct of the foreign relations which were to be Disraeli's main preoccupation and interest in this ministry.

EIGHT

"Beaconsfieldism"

IN DECEMBER 1877 Derby wrote to Salisbury of their chief that "he believes thoroughly in 'prestige' . . . , and would think it (quite sincerely) in the interests of the country to spend 200 millions on a war if the result was to make foreign States think more highly of us as a military power." At the time of Disraeli's death, Lord Acton wrote that in Gladstone's opinion his great rival had "demoralised public opinion, bargained with diseased appetites, stimulated passions, prejudices, and selfish desires, that they might maintain his influence." Gladstone would have had Disraeli's foreign policy, "Beaconsfieldism" as he called it after the title Disraeli acquired in 1876, very much in mind.

Gladstone's opinion, which his close friend Acton accurately summarized, was harsh, but basically accurate. Disraeli did see foreign policy mainly as a tool in party conflict. As he had written to Derby in July 1871:

> I am not . . . sorry to see the country fairly frightened about foreign affairs. 1st, because it is well, that the mind of the nation should be diverted from that morbid spirit of domestic change and criticism, which has ruled us too much

for the last forty years, and that the reign of priggism should terminate. It has done its work, and in its generation very well, but there is another spirit abroad now, and it is time that there shd. be.

2nd. because I am persuaded that any reconstruction of our naval and military systems, that is practicable, will, on the whole, be favorable to the aristocracy, by wh. I mean particularly the proprietors of land: and 3rdly because I do not think the present party in power are well qualified to deal with the external difficulties wh. await them.

Considering that he was writing to one of the prigs, for Stanley's opinions had not changed with his change of title, Disraeli could hardly have made it clearer that he thought a strong and aggressive stance in foreign affairs to the Conservative party's advantage. He acted on his perception of the party's interest both in opposition and in office. And, as Derby, who resumed the post of Foreign Secretary he had held in the previous Conservative administration, had good cause to know, his chief was acutely concerned not only with being, but even more with being seen to be, strong and active abroad. Disraeli was constantly preaching to Derby, to use a favorite phrase of his, that "we must not be afraid of saying 'Bo to a goose.'" He boasted to Lady Bradford in May 1875 that "I believe, since Pam, we have never been so energetic, and in a year's time we shall be more."

To say that Disraeli saw foreign affairs mainly as a field for party maneuver and that he was often as much concerned with appearances as with substance is not, of course, to say that he had no broad notions of the proper course of British policy. He did have, and he had succinctly summed them up for the elder Derby in the autumn of 1866 in commenting on the Canadian situation:

It never can be our pretence, or our policy, to defend the Canadian frontier against the U.S. If the colonists can't, as a general rule, defend themselves against the Fenians, they can do nothing. They ought to be, and must be, strong enough for that. Power and influence we should exercise in Asia; consequently in Eastern Europe, consequently also in Western Europe; but what is the use of these colonial deadweights which *we do not govern?*

He went on to advise: "Leave the Canadians to defend themselves; recall the African squadrons; give up the settlements on the west coast of Africa; and we shall make a saving which will, at the same time, enable us to build ships and have a good Budget."

Such sentiments may seem odd in the man who half a dozen years later was to charge in his Crystal Palace speech:

> If you look to the history of this country since the advent of Liberalism — forty years ago — you will find that there has been no effort so continuous, so subtle, supported by so much energy, and carried on with so much ability and acumen, as the attempts of Liberalism to effect the disintegration of the Empire of England. And, gentlemen, of all its efforts, this is the one which has been the nearest to success. Statesmen of the highest character, writers of the most distinguished ability, the most organised and efficient means, have been employed in this endeavour. It has been proved to all of us that we have lost money by our Colonies. It has been shown with precise, with mathematical demonstration, that there never was a jewel in the Crown of England that was so truly costly as the possession of India. How often has it been suggested that we should at once emancipate ourselves from this incubus! Well, that result was nearly accomplished. When those subtle views were adopted by the country under the plausible plea of granting self-government to the Colonies, I confess that I myself thought that the tie was broken.

Disraeli immediately went on to make clear, however, that he had not the slightest objection to self-government. "I cannot conceive how our distant Colonies can have their affairs administered except by self-government."

But he argued that when self-government was conceded it ought to have been "conceded as part of a great policy of Imperial consolidation." It ought to have been accompanied, he said, by an imperial tariff, by the safeguarding

of the interests of the people of England in unappropri-
ated land, and by agreements for mutual defense. There
ought to have been "the institution of some representative
council in the metropolis, which would have brought the
Colonies into constant and continuous relations with the
Home Government."

> All this, however, was omitted because those who advised
> that policy . . . looked upon the Colonies of England, looked
> even upon our connection with India, as a burden upon this
> country; viewing everything from a financial aspect, and to-
> tally passing by those moral and political considerations
> which make nations great, and by the influence of which
> alone men are distinguished from animals.
>
> Well, what has been the result of this attempt during the
> reign of Liberalism for the disintegration of Empire? It has
> entirely failed. But how has it failed? Through the sympathy
> of the Colonies for the Mother Country. They have decided
> that the Empire shall not be destroyed; and in my opinion
> no Minister in this country will do his duty who neglects any
> opportunity of reconstructing as much as possible our Colo-
> nial Empire, and of responding to those distant sympathies
> which may become the source of incalculable strength and
> happiness to this land.

It has been pointed out by more than one critic that Disraeli subsequently did nothing to implement his suggestions
for the creation of imperial institutions. Buckle, responding to such criticism by Gladstone's biographer John
Morley, remarked that it is "true that many of Disraeli's
most fertile ideas did not issue in Bills; and as a practical
politician he must in this respect yield place to Gladstone."
But, Buckle continues, it is "precisely the fact that Gladstone seldom or never played with political ideas which
could not be enclosed within the compass of a Bill that
marks his inferiority as a statesman and explains his dimin-
ishing hold on the present generation; and it is precisely
the fact that Disraeli did allow his mind such free play
that is his greatest praise in our eyes and that will insure
his fame with those who come after us." The comparison is

unfair to Gladstone, whose libertarian and egalitarian notions were certainly too broad to be encompassed in mere
bills. It is also dated in that in 1920 when it was published
Britain had just emerged from a great struggle in which
the imperial sentiment Disraeli talked about had told enor-
mously to the benefit of the Mother Country, and when
pacific liberalism of the Gladstone variety was out of style.
It is unlikely that many in the present generation would
find as much to praise in Disraeli; but it is undoubtedly
true that, for better or for worse, his fame will rest more
on ideas he popularized than on policies he implemented.
Of these ideas, imperialism is certainly one of the most important.

C. C. Eldridge, in a recent and very able survey of the
idea in the age of Gladstone and Disraeli, has seen Disraeli's
great contribution to its development in his comprehension
of "the possibility of utilising British possessions to increase British influence and power. It was not 'colonial'
policy that Disraeli was interested in but the effect of the
possession of empire on British foreign policy; the empire
was a 'visible expression of the power of England in the
affairs of the world.'" He goes on to credit Disraeli with
popularizing the connection between empire and power,
and for associating the Conservative party with a foreign
policy which stressed these elements.

It is evident that empire was an important ingredient in
Disraeli's policy of prestige; it is also evident that he was
anxious to associate his party and inspire the country with
his notions. As he challenged his Crystal Palace audience,
the question was "whether you will be a great country, an
imperial country, a country where your sons when they rise,
rise to paramount positions, and obtain, not merely the
esteem of your countrymen but command the respect of the
world." Whether, in fact, policies of prestige, policies which
place an at least equal stress on the display of power and
force as on their possession, actually promote real interests

is a question much debated then, and since. But there can be no doubt that Disraeli thought so.

It is also true, as Eldridge suggests, that, while Disraeli talked of the empire as a whole, in practice he drew important distinctions between its several elements. His primary interest was never in the colonies of white settlement, as opposed to India. As it happens, his public rhetoric was fairly consistently favorable to the colonial empire. This was partly because of the close association of protectionist and colonial interests, partly because he had long believed that empire had a prestige value that could be exploited. In practice, however, his attitude had tended to vary depending on whether he was in or out of office. His private anti-colonial remarks, calling the colonies "deadweights" to Derby in 1866 and the famous remark to Malmesbury in 1852 that "these wretched colonies" are "a millstone round our necks," were both made in office, when he was a Chancellor of the Exchequer struggling to balance a budget.

Such remarks were certainly not consistent with the notions of sympathy and sentiment that he later expounded at the Crystal Palace, nor with the ideals of the British Commonwealth of Nations, the later emergence of which owed much to his early perception and popularization of these sentiments, if not much to his practice. But, as the work of Messrs. Robinson and Gallagher has demonstrated, his apparently uncomplimentary remarks about colonies were perfectly consistent with a hard-headed, and in a sense even an imperialistic, policy for the promotion of British power and influence pursued by all governments during the period. It was assumed that in most cases the colonies could and ought to govern and defend themselves. It was also assumed that both affection and interest would continue to bind them to the Mother Country. Thus the institution of colonial self-government, with the burdens that went with it, would be a great saving to the British taxpayer, but would at the same time promote British power and influence. The colonies would bear the expense, and Britain would reap the advantages, not only in actual savings, but in being able to concentrate her limited resources for maximum effectiveness and influence around the globe. Such was the policy Disraeli advocated to the elder Derby; and such was the policy which Conservative governments implemented in their brief tenures of office, most notably in the British North America Act of 1867, which aimed through confederation to make the several British colonies in North America capable of looking after themselves. Disraeli's government would attempt to follow the same policy once again in South Africa, with much less happy results.

The colonies of white settlement in North America, in Africa, and in Australasia, then, should so far as possible be encouraged to look after themselves, and in the process to look after British interests. This was an assumption of all governments during the period, though Disraeli clothed the policy of his government in grander rhetoric. Most governments would have sympathized with the desire which Disraeli expressed to the elder Derby to be rid of the expensive and unrewarding presence in West Africa had public opinion not demanded this continuing commitment to the abolition of the slave trade. All governments agreed that the country's most important overseas possession was that "jewel in the Crown of England," India, and that India could not be expected to look after herself, but on the contrary must be jealously guarded.

Disraeli had told Derby that "power and influence we should exercise in Asia; consequently in Eastern Europe, consequently in Western Europe. . . ." The formulation was distinctive, and particularly distinctive was the stress Disraeli put on the two latter elements in it. Partly from preference, partly from necessity, Gladstone had remained aloof from the affairs of the continent. No leading British statesman, including Disraeli, had foreseen the revolution in the balance of power implicit in Bismarck's policy of

German unification. For the defeat of France in 1871 left Germany the dominant power on the continent. But even if they had foreseen such a consequence, there was little British statesmen could have done about it. The smallness of the British army would have made effective intervention impossible against German military might. Gladstone therefore would have had little choice but to look on while events took their course.

Still Disraeli had a juster appreciation of grand strategy than did Gladstone, and he deserves credit for helping to reverse the tendency toward isolation from continental affairs that had set in under his rival. As has been seen, he was determined to play a part, and equally important to be perceived to play a part, in European questions. He therefore initiated a policy of activity and interference which, as he himself said, was unprecedented since Palmerston's day. Because Bismarck had achieved his objective, and Germany was, as he put it, satiated and therefore anxious to find a new balance, the value of Britain as a makeweight allowed Disraeli to score some minor triumphs in Western European affairs. But the hard considerations of military power, which were not altered in Disraeli's day, remained. It was therefore just as well for him that the attention of all Europe swung to the East, where British power could more easily make itself felt. As a consequence he was able to fulfill his desire to play a great role on the European stage, and to achieve a resounding triumph.

Before Disraeli played his grand role at Berlin, however, he was to make an almost equally dazzling coup, and one of more lasting importance: the purchase of the Suez Canal shares in 1875. The canal, built by a French company and opened in 1869, had profoundly altered the situation in the Middle East, and more particularly the key British concern of access to India. Prior to its opening, the closest sea route to India had been around the Cape of Good Hope. The quicker route through the Mediterranean had traditionally involved debarking on the Syrian coast and traveling overland through Mesopotamia to the Persian Gulf. It was the fact that this route lay through Turkish territory and was closer to Constantinople that had given the Crimean War such apparent urgency. The Suez Canal, much farther west and lying through the territory of a virtually independent Egypt, made the fate of Turkey much less important for the British, though, as will be seen, this was by no means evident to statesmen at the time.

Palmerston's hostility, which Disraeli had shared, had prevented Britain from having anything to do with the building of the canal. Disraeli, however, was keenly anxious to rectify the situation and secure Britain a voice in the management of the Canal Company. When he came to power the time seemed to be ripe, as the company was in financial difficulties; and one of his early acts, in May 1874, was to send the future Lord Rothschild, "Natty" as Disraeli affectionately called him, to Paris to look into the possibility of the government purchasing shares. But the French interests which controlled the company were uninterested, and nothing came of the mission.

In 1875, however, Disraeli's opportunity came in another form, and he seized it. Not only was the company in financial difficulties, so was the Khedive of Egypt, who owned 177,000 of the 400,000 ordinary shares. There was no time to be lost, for the interest on the Egyptian debt was due on 1 December and negotiations were already under way with a French syndicate for the mortgage or sale of the shares. It was a race against the Khedive's bankruptcy and foreign intrigue, and Disraeli entered it with zest. As he wrote breathlessly, and forgetting the usual stilted formality of a Prime Minister's correspondence with his sovereign, to the Queen on 18 November:

> The Khedive now says, that it is absolutely necessary that he should have between three and four millions sterling by the 30th of this month!
> Scarcely breathing time! But the thing must be done.
> Mr. Disraeli perceives, that, in his hurry he has not ex-

pressed himself according to etiquette. Your Majesty will be graciously pleased to pardon him! There is no time to re-write it.

Disraeli's task was no small one. Several of his colleagues, including the cautious Derby, were skeptical of such grandiose and unorthodox strokes. But the arguments against letting the highway to empire, four-fifths of the shipping on which was British, fall further under French influence were compelling ones. His colleagues came round in principle; and Derby warned off the French, who, with the threat of their great neighbor to the east, did not wish to antagonize Britain. There was still the problem of find-ing the money. "I am sure," Northcote, the Chancellor of the Exchequer, wrote to Disraeli on 22 November, "that there is no way we can raise the money without the consent of Parliament, and that the utmost we could do would be to enter into a treaty engaging to ask Parliament for the money, and then let the K[hedive] get it in advance from some capitalist who is willing to trust to our power of get-ting Parliamentary authority."

Disraeli, however, had other ideas; and whether the famous story of the arrangement of the Rothschild loan be literally true or not, it accurately reflects the daring and dramatic flair with which he carried through the whole venture. As Monty Corry later told the tale, he had been waiting at the door of the Cabinet room for a signal from his chief. When the Prime Minister stuck his head out the door and said "Yes," Corry immediately posted off to New Court, where he found Baron de Rothschild at lunch. He informed him that his chief wanted £4,000,000 "tomorrow." Rothschild thereupon picked up a muscatel grape, ate it, spat out the skin, and finally inquired deliberately, "What is your security?" "The British Government." "You shall have it."

Disraeli was cock-a-hoop. He wrote to the Queen on 24 November:

It is just settled: you have it, Madam. The French Government has been out-generaled. They tried too much, offering loans at an usurious rate, and with conditions, which would have virtually given them the government of Egypt.

The Khedive, in despair and disgust, offered your Majesty's Government to purchase his shares outright. He never would listen to such a proposition before.

Four millions sterling! and almost immediately. There was only one firm that could do it — Rothschilds. They behaved admirably; advanced the money at a low rate, and the entire interest of the Khedive is now yours, Madam.

Save in considerably underestimating the French government's willingness to be accommodating, it was a basically accurate summary.

Naturally enough, he was even less restrained in writing to Lady Bradford:

. After a fortnight of the most unceasing labor and anxiety, I (for between ourselves, and ourselves only, I may be egotistical in this matter) — I have purchased for England the Khedive of Egypt's interest in the Suez Canal.

We have had all the gamblers, capitalists, financiers of the world organised and platooned in bands of plunderers, arrayed against us, and secret emissaries in every corner, and have baffled them all, and have never been suspected. The day before yesterday, Lesseps, whose company has the remaining shares, backed by the French Government, whose agent he was, made a great offer. Had it succeeded, the whole of the Suez Canal wd. have belonged to France, and they might have shut it up!

We have given the Khedive 4 millions sterling for his interest, and run the chance of Parliament supporting us. We cd. not call them together for that matter, for that wd. have blown everything to the skies, or to Hades.

The Faery is in ecstasies about "this great and important event." . . .

I have rarely been thro' a week like the last, and am today in a state of prostration — coma. . . .

Disraeli was exaggerating and inaccurate, and not only in the matter of French involvement. As Lord Blake has pointed out, the company could never have shut the canal. That right was always vested ultimately in the government which possessed sovereignty over the territory through which the canal ran, though until our own times it was regulated by international agreements. Even if the company had been able to close the canal, the purchase of only forty-four percent of the shares could hardly have prevented it. Nonetheless the purchase was of immense importance, for a reason given by Cairns, the Lord Chancellor, in a letter to Disraeli:

> It is said — yes, but you cd always have the Canal by war: and even now you must have war all the same.
>
> In the first place there is a large territory *between* peace & war; i.e. negotiation, compromise, influence, pressure etc.; & in this wide territory we shall now be armed with a leverage we never had before.
>
> Then if our rights have to be maintained, of course they must be retained in the last resort by war; & war, *mechanically*, is always the same whatever be the cause. But in our former condition it must have been war to destroy or take possession of the property of others; now it will be a war to defend our own property.

After the opening of the canal, Britain would always have had an overwhelming necessity for intervention in the affairs of Egypt. Now she had the justification. Whether the realities of the world situation which created the necessity were healthy or desirable is open to question. But Disraeli was not responsible for creating them. He had, however, to deal with them. And he did so brilliantly. His was a stroke of boldness, genius, and imagination, and one that advanced real British interests.

It also served another purpose Disraeli had very much at heart. The world was put on notice that Britain was now once again pursuing an active and aggressive foreign policy. As Disraeli told Lady Bradford, the Queen had received a letter from her cousin, the King of the Belgians, congratulating her "on 'the greatest event of modern politics.' 'Europe breathes again,' etc. etc." Her daughter, the Crown Princess of Prussia, enclosed a message from her son, the future Kaiser Wilhelm: "Dear Mama, I must write you a line, because I know you will be so delighted that England has bought the Suez Canal. How jolly!!" The Crown Princess expressed her own opinion that "it is a delightful thing to see the *right thing,* done at the *right moment.*" She also informed her mother that the great Bismarck himself was deeply impressed, a report confirmed by the British Ambassador. Europe was startled and admiring, and Disraeli was exultant.

One reason for Bismarck's interest, and for Disraeli's exultation, was that the news reached Berlin just as the Russian Chancellor, Prince Gortchakoff, on his way back from the spas, stopped off for consultations with the arbiter of Europe. "It must have been during this meeting, or the day before it took place," Disraeli wrote to Lady Bradford, "that the great news arrived, wh., as it is supposed they were going to settle everything without consulting England, was amusing!" What they were going to settle was the Eastern Question.

The Eastern Question, which had already been the cause of much tension and conflict, most notably the Crimean War, was essentially the question of the fate of the Ottoman Empire and of the repercussions on the European, and indeed the world, balance of power. Since the eighteenth century Russia had cast longing eyes toward Constantinople, with its imperial traditions and its promise of access to the western seas; and it was in that century that she began to press the Turks and slowly but surely to nibble away at their territory. Of the other great powers, Prussia had traditionally taken little interest; and, while naturally highly skeptical of the Russian advance, Austria and France had tended to vary in their attitude toward dismemberment depending upon what parts might fall to their lot. Only Britain had pretty consistently opposed partition and seen the empire of the Turks as an essential element in the

stability of the eastern Mediterranean, and, even more important from her point of view, of western Asia and the all-
important access routes to India.

It had therefore been a central element in British policy
to attempt to preserve and prop up the state which in the
nineteenth century became known as the Sick Man of
Europe. In that century, however, a new and ultimately
fatal illness set in — nationalism. From the beginning of the
century, there was unrest and open revolt among the several
Balkan peoples, the Greeks being the first to win their independence in 1830. This had been the great exception to
the rule of British opposition to partition. Canning had
initially been highly skeptical of the Greek cause, but its
success, its popularity in England, and most of all its potential for driving a wedge between the three continental
despotisms, Austria, Prussia, and Russia, brought him
round. For, though the three states were generally united in
their opposition to change, so far as Russia was concerned
the Balkan Peninsula was an exception. As most of the
Balkan peoples were fellow Slavs and also shared a common
religion, Russia looked upon herself as their special protector, a role which was also calculated to advance her
influence in the peninsula. Canning took advantage of
Russian sentiments and appetites to break the so-called
Holy Alliance by joining in encouraging the Greeks, a
policy to which the Goderich and Wellington governments
somewhat uncomfortably adhered. But Palmerston, who
was to be the dominant figure in foreign affairs from 1830
until his death, returned and steadfastly clove to the traditional policy of supporting the Turks.

The most notable instance of this support to date had
been the Crimean War, when Britain and France had
united to check the Russian advance. The Treaty of Paris
of 1856 which concluded the war had attempted to place
stringent safeguards against any future Russian threat,
among them a guarantee by all the great powers of the independence and integrity of the Ottoman Empire, and an

agreement to neutralize the Black Sea and thus prevent Russian naval pressure on the Turks. The effects in the long run of this check administered to Russia had not, however, turned out entirely to British tastes. Checked in the west, the Russians turned their attention eastward and gratified their expansive tastes at the expense, among others, of the khanates 'of central Asia, thus approaching India from another direction. Russia also waited for the first opportunity to reverse the humiliation of 1856. She got it in 1870, in circumstances that clearly illustrated the unfortunate consequences for Britain of the revolution taking place in the European balance of power. France was prostrate after her war with Germany. Bismarck was grateful for Russian neutrality, and Russia seized the chance to repudiate the Black Sea clauses of the Treaty of Paris. Britain and Austria protested; but, when Germany backed Russia, neither was in a position to do much about it. As a consequence a conference in London in 1871, while declaring against unilateral breaches of international agreements, tamely accepted this one by Russia.

In his desire to stabilize the new status quo in Europe, and in view of the natural hostility of France, Bismarck reckoned that the wisest course was to secure agreement and cooperation among the three continental empires of Germany, Austria, and Russia. The result was the so-called Three Emperors' League of 1873. The main cement of the league, however, was simply monarchical solidarity in the face of revolutionary theory, and it became evident that this was a not entirely sound foundation. In the spring of 1875 Russia joined Britain in warning Germany off any further military action against France, which Bismarck had at least been suggesting. This was one of the occasions when Derby was urged to say "Bo to a goose." It was also the occasion on which Disraeli told Lady Bradford that British policy had never been so energetic since Palmerston and would become more so.

In July of 1875 came events that would strain the league

at its weakest point and ultimately give Disraeli the opportunity he craved to play a great role on the European stage.
A revolt against Turkish rule broke out in Herzegovina and
soon spread to Bosnia. The Serbs at once declared their
support of the insurgents. Unrest in the Balkans, particularly on her own southern borders, was bound to unsettle
Austria, and likely to set the Russians to fishing in troubled
waters, which would unsettle her still more. Bismarck was
naturally anxious to prevent this and active in attempting
to maintain good relations between his allies. There was,
therefore, probably some justification for Disraeli's complaint that the three continental powers were attempting to
settle matters without consulting Britain. Basically, however, Disraeli was interested in more than being consulted,
and indeed in more than merely preserving the status quo.
He wanted a great triumph. As he wrote to Lady Bradford
on 3 November: "I really believe 'the Eastern Question,'
that has haunted Europe for a century, and wh. I thought
the Crimean War had adjourned for half another, will fall
to my lot to encounter — dare I say to settle?" And on 10
November, after a strong speech at the Guildhall, he wrote:
" 'Live in a blaze and in a blaze expire!' wd. content me,
but I won't be snuffed out. . . ."

Disraeli's desire to make a grand stroke helps to explain
his government's skepticism of the continental powers' attempts to associate Britain in urging reforms on the Turks,
and its great reluctance to join in a proposal that was therefore drawn up without its being consulted. It is an even
more obvious explanation of the decision to send the fleet
to Besika Bay just outside the Straits, which also took place
in the spring of 1876. Both these actions strengthened the
Turks in setting their faces against reform; and events in
May were to demonstrate that changes in the Turkish governance of subject peoples were desperately required. Revolt had spread to Bulgaria, and Turkish irregulars savagely
put it down with the indiscriminate slaughter of thousands.

Disraeli's reaction to the news of the atrocities, which

began to filter in in June, was unfortunate and got him into serious difficulty. He was not properly informed on the matter, neither the ambassador nor the Foreign Office having done its duty. The fact that the reports of the atrocities came mainly from the Liberal press only added to his natural skepticism and tendency to be sometimes too tolerant of the peculiarities of other cultures, particularly one of which he prided himself that he had firsthand knowledge. Especially memorable for its apparent callousness was a remark made to the House on 10 July:

> I cannot doubt that atrocities have been committed in Bulgaria; but that girls were sold into slavery, or that more than 10,000 persons have been imprisoned, I doubt. In fact, I doubt whether there is a prison accommodation for so many, or that torture has been practised on a great scale among an Oriental people who seldom, I believe resort to torture, but generally terminate their connection with culprits in a more expeditious manner.

He was perhaps thinking of his own youthful experiences in Albania, and had not meant to be amusing. But he was so interpreted, which did a great deal of harm when many of the rumors he dismissed were substantially confirmed. Nor did it do him much good that only 12,000 instead of the originally reported 26,000 had been murdered.

Meanwhile a great popular movement had begun to gather force among those who had believed from the beginning. English Christians, especially Dissenters and High Churchmen, were furious over the barbarous murder of Bulgarian Christians, and during the course of the summer meetings began to be held denouncing the immorality of the Turks and of a foreign policy that supported them. This brought Gladstone out of a self-imposed retirement. He had always believed that the great questions of politics were moral ones. The 1874 election had suggested to him that the people had not grasped this fact, and he had retired in disgust from the leadership of his party. Now it seemed he had been wrong, and he swept down from Hawarden like a prophet of old. His rhetoric — what Disraeli once called his "drenching rhetoric" — issued first from his pen. On 6 September was published the famous pamphlet *The Bulgarian Horrors and the Question of the East*. Its argument is summed up in what are perhaps its best-remembered lines: "Let the Turks now carry away their abuses in the only possible way, namely by carrying off themselves. Their Zaptiehs and their Mudirs, their Bimbashis and their Yuzbachis, their Kaimakams and their Pashas, one and all, bag and baggage shall, I hope, clear out from the province they have desolated and profaned." Thus, to a litany of her own officialdom, Turkey should depart from Christian Europe.

Disraeli dismissed the pamphlet as "of all the Bulgarian horrors, perhaps the greatest." He had already delivered his answer to it almost a month before it was published. On 11 August he had told the House of Commons that, even admitting the atrocities, they could not alter the fact that solemn international agreements to which Britain was a party and which had been renewed as recently as 1871 guaranteed Turkey's independence and territorial integrity. Nor could they alter the crucial British interests which required the preservation of the Turkish buffer:

. . . Those who suppose that England would ever uphold, or at this moment particularly is upholding, Turkey from blind superstition, and from a want of sympathy with the highest aspirations of humanity, are deceived. What our duty is at this critical moment is to maintain the Empire of England. Nor will we agree to any step, though it may obtain for a moment comparative quiet and a false prosperity, that hazards the existence of that Empire.

At the end of the debate, Disraeli walked slowly down the House to the bar, turned and for a moment drank in the whole familiar scene, then retraced his steps and made his exit behind the Speaker's chair. He had uttered his last

words in the House of Commons, and there were those who
had noticed tears in his eyes as he had done so. The next
morning it was announced that the Queen had been pleased
to create her Prime Minister the Earl of Beaconsfield. The
main reasons were age and ill health. Disraeli was in his
seventy-second year, and he was suffering acutely from the
bronchial complaints that had plagued him since the fifties,
and from what would soon be diagnosed as Bright's disease.
He felt that he could no longer stand the strain of leading
the House of Commons, and therefore retired to the less
boisterous and demanding atmosphere of the House of
Lords. When he took his seat at the beginning of the 1877
session he adapted himself, as one observer put it, "as to
the manner born." He had always been a superb actor. His
own reaction was: "I am dead; dead, but in the Elysian
fields."

Even the Elysian fields, however, could not protect him
from the sound and fury of the Bulgarian atrocities agitation. At a great conference in London in December 1876
one speaker proclaimed: "Perish the interests of England,
perish our dominion in India, sooner than we should strike
one blow or speak one word on behalf of the wrong against
the right." Disraeli was determined not to give in to such
pressure, and was equally determined to preserve the interests and empire of England. But he had by no means a
fixed notion of how to do it. Though he publicly proclaimed the old Palmerstonian policy of preserving Turkey,
in private he was open-minded to say the least. In September 1876 he suggested to Derby that Britain might take the
lead in the solution of the Eastern Question by the partition of Turkey, remarking that "our chance of success will
be greater because from us it will be unexpected."

Yet he was not wedded to that policy either. In the spring
of 1877 Salisbury complained that "English policy is to
float lazily downstream, occasionally putting out a diplomatic boathook to avoid collisions"; "the system of never
making a plan beyond the next move is bearing its natural

fruits." Disraeli was resolved to strike a great blow for England, but what should that blow be?

During the autumn of 1876 and the spring of 1877 it was the tendency of British policy to encourage accommodation, resisting Russian demands for armed intervention and the occupation of Turkish territory to assure reforms, while at the same time pressing Turkey to be conciliatory. A conference of the great powers, called on British initiative at Constantinople late in 1876, endorsed the position of Salisbury, the British delegate, that there should be reform without occupation. But Turkey refused to yield; and in April, having secured her flank by an agreement with Austria, Russia declared war and invaded Turkish territory in the Balkans.

Turkish intransigence and the state of public opinion made it impossible that Britain should immediately go to war in behalf of the Turks. There was, however, a growing feeling among a majority of the Cabinet that Russia must be stopped short of seizing or gaining a preponderant influence at Constantinople. Disraeli had explained his own reasoning on the matter to his friend Lord Barrington in October 1876:

> Many in England say, Why not? England might take Egypt, and so secure our highway to India.
> But the answer is obvious, said Lord B[eaconsfield]. If the Russians had Constantinople, they could at any time march their Army through Syria to the mouth of the Nile, and then what would be the use of our holding Egypt? Not even the command of the sea could help us under such circumstances. People who talk in this manner must be utterly ignorant of geography. Our strength is on the sea. Constantinople is the key of India, and not Egypt and the Suez Canal.

The notion that a Russian army could have used Constantinople as a base to seize Egypt seems exaggerated to say the least, and especially peculiar in one who had traveled the route himself.

But Disraeli also had what seem, to modern eyes at any rate, much sounder perceptions. At a November Cabinet,

Gathorne Hardy records Disraeli's suggestion that Britain purchase some Black Sea port, Batoum or Sinope, from Turkey. "What he wants," Hardy wrote, "is a Malta or Gibraltar, which would prevent the Black Sea being a constant threat to our maritime power in the Mediterranean. He is clearly full of anxiety for the future." Disraeli, of course, could hardly have foreseen Russian power as it is today, and in his own time Russia was not a great maritime threat. Nonetheless, his anxiety not to see her in undisputed control of the Black Sea and the Straits was sound.

The fact is, however, that as on so many other matters Disraeli's fertile imagination was throwing out expedients, some good, some bad, and to none of which he was wedded. Barrington recorded his basic objective throughout: "That England should be victorious in diplomacy (and war if necessary, as a matter of course), is Lord B.'s grand object, and will be a splendid consummation to his wonderful career." Disraeli wanted to win, and it did not really matter how.

A consistent policy would admittedly have been difficult. The Queen pressed for strong action. "The Faery writes every day, and telegraphs every hour," Disraeli told Lady Bradford in June 1877. Yet, besides the hostility of public opinion to Turkey, there were serious divisions in the Cabinet. Derby, the Foreign Secretary, was for peace at almost any price. Lord Carnarvon, the Colonial Secretary, and Salisbury, both High Churchmen, were opposed to associating Britain with Turkey in any way; and Northcote agreed with them. It was not until July that the Cabinet could be brought to a unanimous decision that Britain should declare war if Russia took Constantinople. By then, however, the Russian advance had been halted at Plevna.

There the situation remained until 9 December when Plevna fell. Sofia soon followed, and the Russians advanced steadily on Constantinople. Still the Cabinet was not ready to act, and it took the threat of Disraeli's resignation to carry a strong Queen's Speech. On 23 January it was decided to send the fleet to Constantinople. By this time Northcote and, even more important, Salisbury had come round to Disraeli's way of thinking, and only Carnarvon and Derby resigned. Derby, who was Disraeli's oldest political friend and an important link with progressive and liberal opinion, was persuaded to come back when, after reassuring reports from Constantinople, the fleet was recalled. He remained for a while, even after, the reassuring reports having proved unfounded, the fleet was ordered back again.

By the time it arrived, the Russians were already occupying the lines just outside Constantinople. An armistice had also been concluded, however; so it hardly prevented the Russian occupation of the city, though it was, doubtless, an important element in the hard diplomatic bargaining through which in the next few months Britain seized a diplomatic victory out of the jaws of defeat. The first move was the Russian-imposed peace of San Stefano, the terms of which were announced on 3 March. Under its terms, Montenegro was to be enlarged; so was Serbia; and both were to be completely independent of Turkey. Rumania was also to be independent, with Russia taking some of her territory in return for compensation elsewhere. Bosnia and Herzegovina were to be granted reforms. Bulgaria was to be an autonomous state under an elected prince. It was to include most of Macedonia and stretch to the Aegean, and for two years it was to be occupied by Russian troops. Turkey also made large concessions on the southern shores of the Black Sea, where there had also been fighting.

Britain had insisted all along that peace terms must be submitted to a congress of the powers. To this Russia would not agree, and the Cabinet decided to take more forceful measures. These were made easier by the appearance of a public opinion, mainly south of the Trent and particularly in the metropolis, which ran strongly counter to that of the so-called Atrocitarians. Its sentiments are summed up in the famous music-hall ditty:

We don't want to fight, but, by Jingo, if we do,
We've got the ships, we've got the men, we've got
the money too, —

Disraeli was naturally delighted by the turn of events, and entered with zest into the subsequent saber-rattling in which the Cabinet 'felt it necessary to indulge. He was particularly excited over the decision to bring 7,000 Indian troops to Malta, writing to the Queen on 12 April:

> The Cabinet considered this morning the subject of the introduction of your Majesty's Indian Army into the Mediterranean and made many arrangements. Lord Beaconsfield believes this to be a matter of supreme importance. After all the sneers of our not having any great military force, the imagination of the Continent will be much affected by the first appearance of what they will believe to be an inexhaustible supply of men.

Such gestures lost Derby for good, but he was now believed to be dispensable.

The British measures could certainly not have prevented the occupation of Constantinople had the Russians been strong and determined; but the Russian army was exhausted, and government counsels divided. Austria, whose neutrality had been secured by the promise of Bosnia and Herzegovina and the assurance that no large state would be created in the Balkans, was naturally angry over San Stefano, and threw her weight onto the British side. So, by a happy combination of circumstances, bluff and bluster won in the end. The Austrian Foreign Secretary issued invitations for a congress to meet at Berlin; and the Russians, having failed to woo back Austria or to budge Britain, finally agreed to submit the peace terms to it, though in fact the broad outlines of a revised peace had been worked out previously in secret agreements between Russia and Britain.

It was undoubtedly a great victory for Britain, and for her Prime Minister. "England," said his onetime Radical foe J. A. Roebuck, "now holds as proud a position as she

ever held; and that is due to the sagacity, and power, and
conduct of the despised person once called Benjamin Disraeli, but now Lord Beaconsfield." Both claims were in a
sense true. British prestige was indeed at a high point,
though the foundations were weak, and Disraeli deserved a
great deal of the credit. He had been determined from the
beginning that Russia should not have her own way, and
she had not got it.

Beyond that, however, he had never had a policy; and
the policy that triumphed at Berlin was not really his, but
that of the once skeptical Salisbury, who had succeeded
Derby as Foreign Secretary. It was in fact a modified policy
of partition, against which Disraeli had always contended,
at least in public. So far as Britain was concerned, the most
important modification of San Stefano was the vast reduction of Bulgaria. An autonomous Bulgaria was now to have
the Balkan Mountains as its southern boundary. The territory to the south, to be known as Eastern Rumelia, was to
have a special organization, but to remain part of Turkey.
Macedonia was to enjoy certain reforms, but was to be
returned to Turkey without other restrictions. Thus a
Turkish buffer in Europe was to be retained. Salisbury,
however, had little faith in Turkey's long-term prospects.
He therefore proposed that Britain should annex Cyprus
in return for a guarantee of Asiatic Turkey. Disraeli had,
it is true, long had in mind the acquiring of some place of
arms; and in the course of the past several years his fertile
imagination had run from the Black Sea, to the Persian
Gulf, to spots all over the eastern Mediterranean, including
Cyprus. Salisbury, however, certainly had more notion of
what he wanted to do with it, though Disraeli was quite
willing to assure the Queen that "Cyprus is the key to
Western Asia." It was therefore acquired, by a separate
agreement with Turkey before the Congress met.

Salisbury, of course, required, and received, Disraeli's
support throughout. And the Prime Minister cut a fine
figure at the Congress that met in June and July. A

catastrophic beginning was avoided by the diplomacy of the British Ambassador at Berlin, Lord Odo Russell. Disraeli intended to address the opening session in French, and his was so bad that Corry and others close to him were in agonies of apprehension. Lord Odo saved the day, telling him that it would be an immense disappointment to the assembled plenipotentiaries. "They know that they have here in you the greatest living master of English oratory, and are looking forward to your speech in English as the intellectual treat of their lives." He was never entirely sure whether the Prime Minister took the hint or the compliment; but, at any rate, it worked, and Disraeli used English throughout the Congress. He made a tremendous impression. *"Der alte Jude, das ist der Mann,"* was Bismarck's assessment. His usual dramatic flair was apparent. The well-known story about his ordering his special train prepared when the Russians became sticky over some of the terms for Eastern Rumelia and of their giving in almost as the steam built up in the engine must be in part a myth, as they had already decided to concede before he is supposed to have given the order. But there is no question that he threatened to break up the Congress over the matter, and that this brought results. No one can deny that his was a great and glorious performance.

On his return he got a hero's welcome, albeit one partially organized by his old friend Lord Henry Lennox. Amidst cheering crowds, Disraeli and Salisbury drove together from Charing Cross to Downing Street. Both appeared at the windows, and it was then that Disraeli made his famous pronouncement that they had brought back from Berlin "Peace with Honor."

As in other instances where the same claim has been made, it is open to considerable question. Subsequent events were to suggest that Britain would have been much better advised to have put her faith in Balkan, and particularly Bulgarian, nationalism as a bar to the advance of the great neighbor to the north rather than trying to shore up a despotic and corrupt power to the south. Gladstone had some perception of this fact, though, as often happens in such cases, he put his advice in such emotional terms as to be unintelligible to the great majority of responsible politicians. Disraeli can perhaps be criticized more legitimately over Cyprus, which was not to be of much value to him, or anyone else. True, it is difficult to say what might have been if Gladstone's subsequent seizure of Egypt had not made Cyprus irrelevant, at least in the eyes of the statesmen who followed him. But, if Disraeli really believed his public justification — "In taking Cyprus the movement is not Mediterranean, it is Indian" — he was certainly being foolish.

In fact, however, it is difficult to believe that Disraeli had any very serious opinions on the matter one way or the other. More likely his real concerns were reflected in his triumphant boast to Lady Bradford after a rousing speech at the Guildhall in November: "The party is what is called on its legs again, and jingoism triumphant!"

Epilogue and Conclusion

THE TRIUMPH at Berlin was the zenith of Disraeli's career. He was exalted by his friends. An ecstatic Queen bestowed the Garter on him, and by his desire on Salisbury. He also trampled on his enemies, responding to Gladstone's criticisms by publicly calling him "a sophisticated rhetorician, inebriated by the exuberance of his own verbosity, and gifted with an egotistical imagination that can at all times command an interminable and inconsistent series of arguments to malign an opponent and to glorify himself."

Unfortunately for Disraeli, however, the future lay with Gladstone. The causes for the decline of his popularity were largely beyond Disraeli's control. One was the so-called Great Depression, which had begun to set in even before he assumed office and lasted long after he quit it. It was a real depression in agriculture, now for the first time facing vigorous foreign competition brought by the railroad, the steamship, refrigeration, and other technological advances. In trade and industry, it was actually only a depression of prices and profits, but for a large segment of the electorate that was bad enough; and the sense of malaise probably exacerbated cyclical dislocations in the economy and spread suffering a good deal further. Then there were the two disastrous imperial wars, one in Afghanistan, the other in South Africa.

Disraeli had been most amused at Berlin when Bismarck upon hearing of the annexation of Cyprus remarked: "This is progress." "His idea of progress," Disraeli wrote to the Queen, "was evidently seizing something." For all his imperial rhetoric, it was never Disraeli's idea. He loved to exalt the empire, and the monarchy, as in making the Queen Empress of India in 1876: "It is only by the amplification of titles that you can often touch and satisfy the imagination of nations; and that is an element which Governments must not despise." He also loved great flourishes, such as the annexation of Cyprus or the purchase of the Suez Canal shares. But the former he justified only on strategic grounds, to protect an empire Britain already had; and the latter he never saw as the first step toward the acquisition of Egypt. To the contrary, his notion was to continue to share influence there with France, as embodied in the Dual Control of Egyptian finances formally established in 1879. An appetite for the acquisition of territory was not one of Disraeli's vices.

In Afghanistan he was the victim of a reckless Viceroy of India, the Earl of Lytton, the son of his old friend. In view of Russian advances in Asia and intrigue in Afghanistan, threatening the northwest frontier of India, Disraeli was certainly anxious to establish influence there. But Lytton was unnecessarily aggressive in doing so, and managed to involve the country in a costly war, in the course of which the whole British mission at Kabul was murdered in September 1879. Coming close on the heels of the crisis over the Eastern Question, the trouble in Afghanistan was a great embarrassment. As Disraeli remarked to the Indian Secretary in September 1878, so long as the country "thought there was 'Peace with Honor' the conduct of the Government was popular, but if they find there is no peace, they will soon be apt to conclude there is also no honor." It was a prophetic remark. His other famous remark on Lytton's activities was: "When V-Roys . . . disobey orders, they ought to be sure of success in their mutiny."

Disraeli can perhaps be accused of weakness in not removing Lytton, but short of that there was actually little he could do to control him. In places as far away as India, the man on the spot of necessity had great independence; and once he had committed the country to a course of action, it was often almost impossible to reverse. The same considerations apply even more strongly to South Africa. Once again Disraeli can be accused of weakness and, because of preoccupation with other matters, of indifference. Yet when there was no telegraph to Capetown, and telegrams by way of the Cape Verde Islands took two or three weeks to arrive, it would have been difficult with the best will in the world to control the situation there.

In South Africa there was a good deal of justification for the policy pursued; the problem was that it was pressed forward too fast. Besides the British colonies at the Cape and Natal, there existed two semi-independent Boer republics, the Orange Free State and the Transvaal, farther inland. Save in foreign affairs, the two latter were free to do largely as they pleased, and they had particularly bad relations with the native population. As a consequence, the Boers often precipitated disturbances with which the British ultimately had to deal. Carnarvon, until his resignation in 1878 the Colonial Secretary, was anxious to implement a policy of federation, which he had pursued with great success in Canada in the previous Conservative administration. To bring the whole area under one government made good sense, and Carnarvon was sure it would be popular with all concerned. Unfortunately, Carnarvon and his representatives on the spot, Sir Theophilus Shepstone and Sir Bartle Frere, were so sure that their policy ought to be popular that they pressed it forward despite the fact that it clearly was not. In 1877 Shepstone annexed the Transvaal over strong Boer protests. Carnarvon resigned the next year;

but Frere remained as High Commissioner, and he proved to be very much another "man on the spot." Frere turned his attention to the native question, and was especially determined to tame the warlike Zulus. The first consequence was the disaster at Isandhlwana. On 14 February the news reached London that Cetywayo's Zulus had slaughtered to a man a British invading force of 1,300. It was a terrible humiliation, and the beginning of a war that lasted until September.

The Zulu War was hardly over when the news came of the disaster at Kabul. Disraeli's luck had gone sour. In November and December, Gladstone, doing some preliminary campaigning in the Scottish constituency of Midlothian, launched in earnest his great public crusade against Beaconsfieldism in all its forms. As only Gladstone could, he denounced his rival's policies as immoral, and incidentally expensive. In his own eyes, he was fighting the battle of "justice, humanity, freedom, law." Disraeli told Lady Bradford that "I have not read a single line of all this row, but Monty has told me something, and has promised to make notes, in case it fall to my lot to notice his wearisome rhetoric."

The electorate was more impressed. By the end of the 1880 session the Parliament elected in 1874 would have run its statutory limit, and it was originally intended to let it do so. But the heating up of the Home Rule agitation in Ireland, under the brilliant leadership of Charles Stewart Parnell, changed the government's mind. Disraeli had always reckoned that Ireland was a good Conservative issue; and on the same day that the dissolution was announced, 8 March, he attempted in a letter to the Lord Lieutenant to concentrate the attention of the country there. "A portion of its population is attempting to sever the Constitutional tie which unites it to Great Britain in that bond which has favoured the power and prosperity of both." He proclaimed that "the strength of this nation depends on the unity of feeling which should pervade the United Kingdom and its widespread dependencies." It was an appeal which would work for others in the future, but it did not work now. There was doubtless some truth in Disraeli's own assessment that he was beaten by "hard times." But there is also every reason to believe that a large portion of the electorate would have seen politics very much as Gladstone did. At any rate, Disraeli was badly beaten. The new Parliament contained 349 Liberals, 243 Conservatives, and 60 Home Rulers. The Queen parted sadly with her favorite Prime Minister, and after some maneuvering, made possible by the fact that Gladstone had resigned the official leadership, finally had to accept the inevitable.

Disraeli was seventy-six when he left office, and he was to survive his downfall by almost exactly one year. He was by no means crestfallen, and indulged in his usual retirement pastime of writing a novel, or in this case finishing one that had long been abandoned. *Endymion* was the story of a young unknown who through the support and influence of women rose to be Prime Minister. He entered politics just about the same time as Disraeli himself and achieved his ambition in the mid-fifties, and the book has the usual brilliance and fascination of the author's political portraiture. But the Queen was rather puzzled to find that the hero was a Whig; and Archbishop Tait confided to his diary: "I have finished *Endymion* with a painful feeling that the writer considers all political life as mere play and gambling."

In fact, Disraeli was never more statesmanlike than in his last year. Like Wellington and the elder Derby before him, he played a restraining role in the Lords, preventing them from wrecking the government program, and thus precipitating a crisis which could only have been to their own disadvantage. He had warned a party meeting in May 1880:

As to the Constitution, he would not criticise the probable domestic action of the party in power as to particular measures. But there could be no doubt that the first step towards any organic change must be a revolution in the tenure of land — in other words the pulling down of the aristocracy, which was the first object of the revolutionary party. All their propounded schemes should be examined with reference to that keynote.

One could almost have believed in the sessions of 1880 and 1881 that the safety of the aristocracy had been Disraeli's main concern all along. No doubt there had been a fruitful partnership, but that is not quite the same thing.

Though he had continued to live in Whitehall Gardens for a while as Premier, its steep staircase had got too much for him and he had given up the house and moved to Downing Street. Thus his fall from power had left him once more homeless. Again, the Rothschilds came to his aid. His old friend Baron Lionel was dead; but his son Alfred put at his disposal a self-contained set of rooms in his own magnificent house in Seamore Place, tactfully allowing him as much or as little company as he chose. Disraeli, however, wanted a house of his own. Longmans had paid him £10,000 for *Endymion,* so money was no problem, and he secured one at 19 Curzon Street, where he moved in January 1881. It was there that he died. His last words were enviable: "I had rather live, but I am not afraid to die." Early on the morning of 19 April, he half raised up in bed and stretched himself out in a manner that suggested to the faithful Corry the one he always assumed on rising to reply in a debate. The lips moved, but no words came out. Fifteen minutes later he was dead.

He was buried in the Hughenden churchyard, beside Mary Anne. Among the wreaths that had covered the coffin, there were two from his sovereign. One was entirely of fresh primroses, with the inscription: "His favourite flowers, from Osborne, a tribute of affection from Queen Victoria." With him in the coffin, next to his heart, was a farewell letter Mary Anne had written him twenty-five years before.

Disraeli's memory has not paled with the passing years. Indeed, in many ways it has grown more bright; and in the mid–nineteen seventies his name remains one to conjure with. Thus, almost as this is being written, headlines in a leading British Sunday newspaper announce that MIDDLE-WAY TORIES LOOK TO DISRAELI. And it was not many years ago that American newspaper readers found both their President and Secretary of State proclaiming themselves "Disraelian Conservatives" in domestic affairs.

Disraeli's attraction for his fellow countrymen is not far to seek. More than once in the recent past, those within the Conservative party who have wished to resist tendencies toward laissez-faire and a reassertion of the virtues of the free market economy have invoked his name. In 1947 it was Anthony Eden, stating the position of the party leadership against a recalcitrant right wing, who reminded the Conservative Party Conference that "we are not the Party of unbridled, brutal capitalism, and never have been. Although we believe in personal responsibility and personal initiative in business, we are not the political children of the laissez-faire school. We opposed them decade after decade." And two years later Winston Churchill himself would assure Conservatives that the welfare state and managed economy policies which emerged from that conference were in the tradition of the "Tory democracy of Lord Beaconsfield and after him of Lord Randolph Churchill."

Two decades later, it is Mrs. Thatcher who is being delicately reminded. But, according to the *Observer* report of a speech by Peter Walker, Disraeli is once again "enlisted as the man who saw that it was the duty of governments to intervene against social evils created in the mid–nineteenth century, 'when free market forces were triumphant.'" Whoever the adversary, Disraeli is called upon to vindicate moderate, progressive Toryism. He has become firmly part of the tradition which the same report (21 September 1975), with more regard to alliteration than exhaustiveness, describes as that of "Butler, Baldwin, Beaconsfield, Burke and . . . Bolingbroke."

Quite what President Nixon and Dr. Kissinger have to

do with this tradition may not be readily apparent. In an article in the *New York Times Magazine* in 1973 Professor J. H. Plumb speculated that it was perhaps more Disraeli's advocacy of a strong foreign policy which appealed to them. The appropriation of "peace with honor" to describe the Vietnam settlement would seem to add credence to such a view. And Disraeli's preference for a policy of interest, as opposed to morality or sentiment, would undoubtedly have a strong appeal for one, like Dr. Kissinger, brought up in the school of diplomatic history of which William Langer was the archpriest and Harvard the great shrine. All three share an admiration for Metternich.

There is, however, also a tradition in American domestic politics, and also closely connected with the neighborhood of Boston and with academia, of which Dr. Kissinger and others of the former President's close advisers may well feel a part. James MacGregor Burns, among others, has seen Franklin Roosevelt "as a conservative acting in the great British tradition." And Burns goes on to suggest in explanation of New Deal policies that "for over a century conservatives in Britain had been demonstrating, through such reforms as factory acts and social welfare services, that minor changes in institutions and laws were necessary to conserve enduring ends." Since the Roosevelt years those holding such views have placed themselves at the service of both political parties, and both American liberalism and American conservatism have therefore been influenced by a tradition of which Tory Demoracy is a prominent element. To what end and how well the lessons have been learned is doubtless debatable. But that both sides believe themselves to have been influenced is evident.

Disraeli's reputation with posterity as a social reformer and an opponent of laissez-faire largely explains the ups and downs of esteem in which he has been held since his death. On the first anniversary of his passing some of his admirers initiated the custom of wearing primroses in their buttonholes. The idea took hold, and from it grew the

Primrose League, an effort by the Fourth Party of Lord Randolph Churchill to give the Conservative party an organized popular following, and to popularize the ideas associated with Disraeli's name. The league was reasonably successful in the former respect, but Tory Democracy did not flourish. The party of Salisbury and Balfour was not receptive to a program of social reform. During the decade of uninterrupted Tory rule from 1895 to 1905, less was accomplished than in the single session of 1875, only three or four measures of real importance. And some of those, especially the Workmen's Compensation Act of 1897, owed more to the waning radicalism of Joseph Chamberlain than to any tradition indigenous to Conservatism.

For Chamberlain was not typical of the recruits who had been flowing into the party in an ever-growing trickle from midcentury, one which turned into a mighty deluge on Gladstone's conversion to Home Rule in 1886. Conservatism became the haven of frightened landowners and businessmen concerned for the sanctity of their property; and, whatever modern Conservatives may like to believe, the party did become preeminently the party of capitalism and laissez-faire. The change is epitomized in the accession of Andrew Bonar Law to the leadership in 1911. Bonar Law was a wealthy iron merchant, a North American by birth, and one who, in the words of his biographer Lord Blake, "personally believed that, for the Conservatives, social reform was not on the whole a profitable line to pursue."

What had seemed to prove more profitable to the party was the advocacy of a united and powerful empire, and here one might think Disraeli would have come into his own. Such, however, was not the case. Partly no doubt it was because Irish Home Rule, which was the first and probably the most profitable form that the issue took, did not really become of paramount importance until after Disraeli's death. And the later policy of aggressive and expansive imperialism could find better spokesmen and heroes than Disraeli. The generation of Chamberlain and Roseberry, Rhodes and Kitchener, was clearly not lacking in either. Thus, while Gladstone remained an ideal to the political left, a hero in death as well as in life, Disraeli seemed quickly to have become irrelevant.

Gladstone's reputation may have benefited from the fact that John Morley's great biography followed his death by only a few years, coming out in 1903. Monypenny's first volume did not appear until 1910, almost thirty years after its subject's death. But there is surely irony in the fact that that volume provided the occasion for a bitter attack on Disraeli's memory by a great imperialist and a leading Conservative, Lord Cromer, who had made his reputation in Egypt of all places. Cromer wrote him off as a mere adventurer, without principles or objectives. To such depths had Disraeli fallen, unhonored by those who would seem to have owed him most.

And Gladstone was undoubtedly a prophet more appropriate to the general spirit of the age. A generation which launched a war to end all wars and to make the world safe for democracy would certainly have found more inspiration in him than in Disraeli. He had to wait for a more skeptical and less serious age. It was really Philip Guedalla who rediscovered Disraeli. In three essays written in the early postwar years, he examined him as a statesman, a novelist, and a journalist. In the first capacity, Guedalla comments that

> it is possible in the cold dawn of the present century to forget Disraeli's fantastic parades across proud and peacock-haunted parterres, and to estimate his true value and business in English politics. Although it is a figure which appeals irresistibly to the undergraduate imagination with its suggestion of a belated D'Orsay or a premature Randolph Churchill, it is a career with a more serious value for politicians. Disraeli was to some extent the Treitshke [*sic*] of British Imperialism; and on the side of party politics he produced a strain of Toryism which approached almost to the possession of ideas. It may be true that those ideas were either Radical or wrong; but it was a unique achievement to have brought the Country party within thinking range of anything.

And

And Disraeli as a writer of fiction suggested comparison with modern politicians. Having quoted from Disraeli the novelist, Guedella wondered of recent Conservative ex-Chancellors of the Exchequer: "Could Mr. Bonar Law do as much? . . . When Mr. Chamberlain gives us the novel which we have so long looked for, one wonders wistfully whether it will begin quite like that."

One suspects that it was not only because, unlike Bonar Law and Austen Chamberlain, Stanley Baldwin had not been Chancellor of the Exchequer that he was excluded from Guedella's speculations. Anyone less likely to have produced a novel is difficult to imagine. Yet it was Baldwin at the 1928 party conference who exhorted his followers to strive for "a further period of ordered progress in the traditions of that greatest of our leaders who we are all so proud to follow — Lord Beaconsfield."

Baldwin was always quoting Disraeli, and it was not mere lip service. As Lord Blake has remarked, "He had an idea, at times cloudy and indistinct yet none the less effective, of the image of Conservatism which he wished to project before the eyes of the electorate. It was that of Disraeli's 'One Nation.' Baldwin discerned that the British — or perhaps it is safer to say the English — people are not by nature addicted to class warfare." And doubtless it was the fact that in the nineteen twenties, the decade of severe economic dislocation and the General Strike, class war loomed as a real and apparent danger that made Disraeli once again seem particularly relevant. Certainly, it has since been at times of acute social tension and strife that his image has seemed most bright. And his name and example have served a succession of Conservative leaders anxious to accommodate their party to the times, and carry measures to soften and blur class antagonisms. As has been seen, his memory has played a not dissimilar role in America.

Does Disraeli deserve the reputation he has attained with posterity? Clearly there were those among his contemporaries who drew a similar meaning from his life. John Gorst, another member of the Fourth Party who knew him well, believed, as we have seen, that he had been dedicated to the ideal of Tory Democracy. Randolph Churchill, who coined the label, said not long after Disraeli's death that his phrase *"Sanitas, sanitatum, omnia sanitas"* expressed the "schème of social progress and reform" of Tory Democracy.

Disraeli's serious biographers have differed on the question. No one has ever taken Tory Democracy at face value, or believed that the classes are quite as altruistic in the pursuit of the interests of the masses as its theories suggest. But allowing for the fact that politics are almost always a mixture of interest and idealism, Monypenny and Buckle would take the view of the Tory Democrats. They would largely accept the interpretation promulgated by Disraeli himself at the end of his life, seeing him as the champion of old institutions, of the people, and of a strong foreign and imperial policy based firmly on British interests. It is true, and here lies the work's enduring greatness, that there is no subsequent interpretation of Disraeli's career that its authors have not anticipated. In the finest tradition of nineteenth-century historiography, all the arguments and masses of evidence are marshaled for the reader. Never, however, does the author's line of interpretation become obscure; Monypenny and Buckle remain in control.

The same cannot be said of the most recent biography by Lord Blake. Like its predecessor, it is a gold mine of information, it has incorporated subsequent scholarly work, and it has some fine passages. But the interpretation is murky. Until the leadership of the party in the Commons was substantially secured in 1849, Blake portrays Disraeli essentially as an unprincipled opportunist. Then, as we have seen, he suggests that the theme which holds together Disraeli's political life is his devotion to the aristocratic settlement, the dominance of English society and politics by the greater landowning classes. For Blake, this excludes what might be called the Tory Democratic interpretation, which he believes that Randolph Churchill concocted for his own purposes. And Blake believes that Disraeli was actually convinced that the aristocratic Jewish background he dreamt up for himself gave him a special kinship with, and even superiority to, the English aristocracy.

What is the truth of the matter? It would have been very strange indeed if the man who for thirty years led the party of the landed classes had not had many flattering things to say about its leading members. There can be no doubt whatever that he considered himself more than their equal, as the *un*flattering remarks he made about them prove. Neither did he ever attempt to hide, or apologise for, the fact that he was a Jew — apart from anything else he was too sensible and too much a realist for that. But, as the preceding chapters have one hopes made evident, neither in a belief in aristocracy, nor in this version of the influence upon him of his Jewishness, can one find an integrating thread in Disraeli's life.

Even less can one find it in Cecil Roth's version, which takes seriously Disraeli's commitment to tolerant and progressive Toryism, and sees it as conditioned by his Jewishness and by his resulting sympathy with the poor and oppressed. It is true that Disraeli flung Jewish emancipation in the face of friend and foe alike. But though he favored civic and political equality for Jews, he took pains to make clear that he did not argue for it on liberal grounds. If any further proof were needed, his own exploitation of religious bigotry against Catholics, Ritualists, and Dissenters whenever it suited his political purposes would provide it. It is difficult to believe that Disraeli felt any special kinship with the downtrodden.

Gladstone's approach was probably sounder than any discussed thus far. It fell to Gladstone's lot as Leader of the House to deliver a eulogy after his great rival's death. It cost him much anguish and a severe attack of diarrhea, but he finally did it. He talked not of Disraeli's principles and policies, but of his personal characteristics: "his strength of will; his long-sighted consistency of purpose, reaching from his first entrance upon the avenue of life to its very close; his remarkable power of self-government; and last, but not least of all, his great parliamentary courage. . . ."

Gladstone did not elaborate, but one may perhaps do it for him. Disraeli's strength of will and consistency of purpose were concentrated on one end, the advancement of his own ambitions. The power of self-government he exercised in the suppression of any act or feeling that might stand in the way. And his courage was of the sort required to do anything, however much it might be opposed to past stands and promises, necessary to secure his end. Whatever its merits as a general explanation of politics, the interpretation of that historical school associated with the name of Maurice Cowling fits Disraeli perfectly. For him, politics was a perpetual jockeying for power and place, and little else. It is quite appropriate that he should have been the archetypal figure for the Cowlingites.

Shortly after Disraeli's death, Lord Lytton wondered how the unborn biographer could know of the man's whole character, and all his lovable sides; his warmth of heart, domestic tenderness, filial piety, and loyalty to friends; his freedom from malice and vindictiveness. In fact, all these characteristics do strike the modern biographer. Undoubtedly, to those who loved him, or at least did not get in his way, he could be a most lovable character.

But one must also be struck by the self-centeredness, the immense egocentricity that marked Disraeli's personal relationships. The public man evokes the same kind of mixed reaction. One can hardly fail to be impressed with the sympathy and understanding with which Disraeli was able to enter into the sufferings, and to a certain extent the aspirations, of workingmen. His perception of the degradation imposed by the Master and Servant Laws upon workers, for example, was as keen as anyone's could have been who did not suffer under it. Yet even Monypenny was forced to admit that "self-worship was often, no doubt, in conflict with that surrender to a great purpose which we associate with the highest greatness." And one cannot but feel that it is just as well for his reputation as a social reformer that such a stance was always conducive to his political interest, rather than varying; as, for example, did the usefulness of exploiting bigotry and intolerance, phenomena which he certainly understood equally well.

Monypenny remarks of Disraeli early in his career that far from having no convictions, Disraeli had too many, and that this is what got him into difficulty. It would perhaps be more accurate to say that he had a conviction for every occasion. Some were bound to be good, some bad. Several have been of great significance. The religious passions he helped to fan still flame in Northern Ireland. Jingoism only died, appropriately enough, at Suez. The Commonwealth ideals which he helped to foster would seem to have an uncertain future, his concern for Europe a rather brighter one.

It is, however, those of his notions which gave rise to so-called Tory Democracy that posterity has chosen mainly to remember. No doubt the Reform Act of 1867 was in retrospect the critical step in the founding of modern democracy in Britain. No doubt too his social policies did much to fix in men's minds, on both sides of the Atlantic, the state's responsibility for the welfare of all its citizens. Disraeli's is perhaps an example of the good men do living after them.